17 Reasons to Admire Birds

Val Shushkewich

Published by Val Shushkewich, 2022.

While every precaution has been taken in the preparation of this book, the publisher assumes no responsibility for errors or omissions, or for damages resulting from the use of the information contained herein.

17 REASONS TO ADMIRE BIRDS

First edition. January 17, 2022.

Copyright © 2022 Val Shushkewich.

ISBN: 979-8201498535

Written by Val Shushkewich.

Table of Contents

PREFACE

We can learn a great deal about the best way to live our lives from observing the birds. Although the goals of birds—to survive in the natural world and to further their species—are straightforward, in many ways these goals are not easy to attain. In striving to attain their goals, birds have developed an admirable suite of characteristics and behaviors. From courageously trying to drive off dangerous predators to undertaking mind-boggling migrations to find the best conditions for raising their families, birds try their hardest to succeed.

Watching how birds conduct themselves teaches us many valuable lessons about the best qualities to have in life. This book demonstrates how birds show positive qualities. It combines the personal experiences of a bird lover with scientific studies about birds' behaviors.

What would the world be like without birds in all their varieties and their complex behaviors? In the past, birds have adapted to changing conditions on earth, and undoubtedly, they will do their best to continue to do so in the future. But humans have altered their environments so much that it may be difficult for them to adapt quickly enough.

The first step to making positive changes that impact the lives of birds is to admire them, to become aware of their needs, and to see how the actions of humans have affected their lives.

A bird lover is someone who pays attention to birds and who notices what they are doing. It is someone who sees a bird in the field and who, once arriving back home, consults field guides to see what kind of bird it is. It is someone whose curiosity about this bird leads to researching its life history. It is someone who believes that birds are extraordinary in their ability to fly long distances and to survive in the natural world unaided by any human-invented comforts. It is someone who believes the world is a more welcoming place because of the birds.

Chapter 1 – Make Every Day Count and Keep It Simple

"The art of being happy lies in the power of extracting happiness from common things."

Henry Ward Beecher

"Happiness is the art of learning how to get joy from your substance."

Jim Rohn

"A happy man is too satisfied with the present to dwell too much on the future."

Albert Einstein

"Each morning when I open my eyes, I say to myself: I, not events, have the power to make me happy or unhappy today. I can choose which it shall be. Yesterday is dead, tomorrow hasn't arrived yet. I have just one day, today, and I'm going to be happy in it."

Groucho Marx

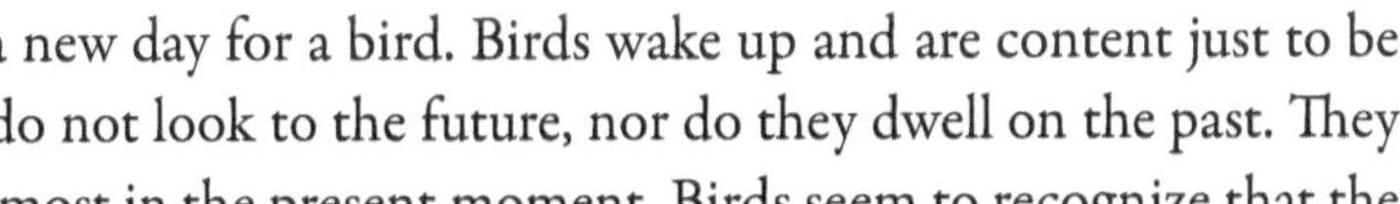

Every day is a new day for a bird. Birds wake up and are content just to be alive. They do not look to the future, nor do they dwell on the past. They do what matters most in the present moment. Birds seem to recognize that the very act of being alive is a gift to be appreciated.

Birds are straightforward. Perhaps their motto could be stated as KISS (Keep It Simple Stupid). They have clear priorities and work with a dominant purpose— to carry on their species. In order to survive and fulfill their purpose, they must find food, maintain their feathers, rest, and be wary of predators by remaining observant and vigilant of their surroundings.

Birds live in harmony with nature and leave a light footprint on the earth. They go about their business without disrupting the balance of the natural environment where they live. They make use of the objects in their natural environment but leave the earth undamaged by their presence. They only take what they need—seeds and berries to eat; twigs and grass to build a nest. Birds seek merely to live in the natural world. This contrasts with humans who often seek to control and dominate nature, in the process altering the environment and upsetting the ecological balance.

Birds make their presence known in simple ways, such as by singing and having beautiful feathers. The simplicity of the way that birds live is captured in the translation of the poem "How Simple": [Ref 1-1]

> "A sweet chirp would suffice
> To let it be known
> That I am here.
> A dropped feather would suffice
> To let the world know
> That I was here.
> The warmth of brooding would suffice
> To testify
> That I will be here.
> How else do birds
> Articulate life
> With greater simplicity?"

We can learn many lessons from the birds, but the most important lesson we can learn is to value these amazing creatures, who add so much interest and beauty to the world, while demanding nothing of us in return. Emily Dickinson's poem *Hope is the thing with feathers* describes her thoughts on a singing bird [Ref 1-2]

Hope is the thing with feathers
That perches in the soul,
And sings the tune without the words,
And never stops at all,
And sweetest in the gale is heard;
And sore must be the storm
That could abash the little bird
That kept so many warm.
I've heard it in the chilliest land,
And on the strangest sea;
Yet, never, in extremity,
It asked a crumb of me.

Chapter 2 –Try to Adapt and Be Flexible

"It is not the strongest of the species that survives, nor the most intelligent. It is the one that is most adaptable to change...The most important factor in survival is neither intelligence nor strength but adaptability."

Charles Darwin

"All failure is failure to adapt, all success is successful adaptation......If they lacked flexibility, they wouldn't be able to adapt to different situations. When you're flexible, you're willing to consider the best approach for each particular situation."

Max McKeown

"Intelligence is ongoing, individual adaptability. Adaptations that an intelligent species may make in a single generation, other species make over many generations of selective breeding and selective dying."

Octavia E. Butler

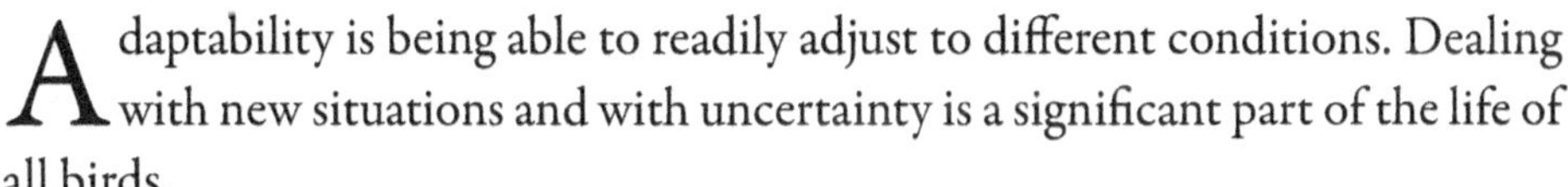

Adaptability is being able to readily adjust to different conditions. Dealing with new situations and with uncertainty is a significant part of the life of all birds.

Birds are capable of adapting to changes in their environment in a number of ways. Over their individual lifetimes, they may respond by altering their behavior. Longer-term adaptations may require changes made over many generations.

The ability to change behavior in response to changes in the environment is known as phenotypic plasticity. An example of this flexibility is birds' laying their eggs earlier to coincide with an earlier appearance of abundant prey for their young. This involves the birds' realizing that warmer temperatures occurring earlier in the spring mean that seasonal prey will appear earlier and therefore the birds must lay their eggs earlier so that their nestlings will hatch at the right time to have the greatest abundance of food.

Scientists used data from a 51-year long-term study on Great Tits breeding in Wytham Woods near Oxford in the United Kingdom to model how birds can match their breeding timing each year to the time when food is most plentiful for their nestlings, and how this match can change with a changing climate. [Ref 2-1] Successful reproduction in Great Tits largely depends on coordinating offspring food demand with a brief annual peak in caterpillar abundance. This can be achieved by individual birds adjusting their laying date to early spring temperatures, which predict the timing of the peak in food availability. Repeated observations of breeding females showed that they advanced their laying dates to coincide with earlier warmer spring temperatures. When the temperature increased by one degree centigrade, which meant that the caterpillars would begin emerging earlier, the birds responded by laying their eggs five days earlier. This meant that their offspring continued to hatch to the peak abundance of caterpillars in their environment. This high phenotypic plasticity of the parent birds allowed them to change their behavior to benefit their offspring's survival.

Birds have evolved structural adaptations that allow them to live in different habitats on the earth. A structural adaptation is a characteristic of an organism that improves its chances of surviving and reproducing. These adaptations are a result of the genes inherited from their parents. The proportion of well-adapted organisms in a population can increase over the generations through the process of evolution by natural selection.

Different species of birds have evolved special characteristics that help them to survive in their unique places in their environment. Those physical and behavioral characteristics that get passed along from generation to generation are the traits that best help them to survive. Birds' beaks, feet, and feather shape have all evolved to be best adapted for the lives that different species of birds lead. An example is the longer, narrower, and more pointed flight feathers on birds that migrate versus those who don't. Air resistance is minimized with longer, more pointed wings.

FIGURE 2-1 – ADULT Barn Swallow. Barn Swallows fly from North American breeding grounds to wintering areas in Central and South America. Image by 16081684 from Pixabay.

The High Arctic in the winter is an extraordinarily challenging environment. Adult Snowy Owls are adapted to survive the coldest winters there. They are among the largest of the owls. Their large size is an advantage in a cold climate as they have more body mass to generate heat and less surface area to let heat escape. Their thick feathers—extending over all parts of their body including their face, legs and toes—are white to help them blend into the Arctic landscape.

A saltmarsh is another extremely challenging habitat. Birds who live in a saltmarsh are exposed to high levels of salt both in their food and in their drinking water. Saltmarsh ecosystems also change from day to day, even hour to hour, on cycles dictated by the tides. For birds living in the marsh, their home will be completely submerged under water for a few days every month when the moon is closest to the earth. Saltmarshes are also filled with abrasive vegetation like cordgrass that wears on feathers. There are no trees, so saltmarsh birds are exposed to harsh sun and high temperatures. Even though it fills with ocean tides, a saltmarsh ecosystem is actually akin to a desert in terms of lack of freshwater and high exposure to sun. Altogether, saltmarshes are a most unwelcome environment for many living things. [Ref 2-2]

Why do bird live in a saltmarsh at all? Jennifer Walsh, the lead author of a recent study of four different sparrow species living in this challenging environment explained: "Sometimes birds move into marshes because, if you can adapt to the environment, it's actually a pretty good place to be. There's no competition because so few species live there, and there is never a shortage of insects for food." [Ref 2-3]

The study of the four different sparrow species living in this challenging environment found that the birds have evolved different species-specific ways to address the same problem of living in a salt-water versus fresh-water environment. They evolved four separate, complex mechanisms to deal with salt, each likely governed by many genes working in tandem.

"For tidal saltmarsh species, the challenge is how to maintain the right balance between water and salt concentrations in their cells," explained Walsh. "When cells are exposed to salt water, they shrink. If they're exposed to too much fresh water, they expand. Without the right balance, the cells can die." (Ref 2-4)

Researchers studied the genomes of four sparrow species: Savannah, Nelson's, Song, and Swamp Sparrow. Each of these species has a population living in a saltmarsh habitat as well as a separate upland population, making it possible to compare the genomes of the two populations and see where they differ. Some of those differences are tied to adaptations that evolved in saltmarsh-resident sparrows to control the balance of water and salt concentrations—a process called osmoregulation.

One gene that appears important in Savannah Sparrows plays a role in inserting physical channels in the cells. Those channels help the cells resist expansion and contraction from changes in salt levels by allowing exchange of water across the cell membrane. Swamp Sparrows show a similar response to salt water, but the genes responsible for forming these channels are completely different. Song Sparrows seem to have adapted through mechanisms that reinforce cell membranes so they can expand and contact more quickly in response to salt. The Nelson's Sparrow takes yet another route—evolving a gene that changes its behavior. Their genetic adaption curbs thirst so they drink only the least amount of salt water necessary and salt levels are kept within bounds.

The researchers also found that these osmoregulatory adaptations evolved at a rapid pace (at least on an evolutionary scale)—probably over the past 10,000 to 15,000 years—and that New World sparrows have colonized marshes over and over again. [Ref 2-5]

Examples of changes occurring over many generations of birds might involve the migratory patterns of bird species. Migratory birds travel north and south annually and have done this in North America since the Ice Age. These migrations have evolved to adapt to changing conditions.

Many birds undertake amazing migration journeys. They may fly tremendous distances, sometimes non-stop over thousands of miles of open ocean in the fall, returning in the spring by entirely different routes. No-one knows the complete story of how they find their way across a featureless ocean. The Pacific Golden Plover flies 2,400 miles across the Pacific Ocean from Alaska to Hawaii each fall, finding its destination without error.

Asiatic birds migrating between Siberia and India cross the 20,000 ft peaks of the Himalayan Mountains. Whimbrels migrate between Arctic nesting areas and wintering grounds as far south as Bolivia, sometimes having to skirt hurricanes as they fly over open ocean.

The daunting migrations of a Whimbrel named Hope were tracked for several years. [Ref 2-6] Hope was one of seven Whimbrels tagged by biologists in 2008 and 2009 as part of a joint project between The Nature Conservancy and the Center for Conservation Biology (CCB) of the College of William and Mary. She was originally captured and fitted with a 9.5-gram satellite radio transmitter on 19 May 2009 while she was making a migratory stopover at Boxtree Creek, a saltwater marsh on the Delmarva Peninsula on the eastern shore of Virginia. She left Virginia on 26 May and flew to the western shore of James Bay where she staged for three weeks before flying to the Mackenzie

River Delta and then on to the Beaufort Sea of the Arctic Ocean. She remained on her breeding territory for more than two weeks before flying again to Hudson Bay. Hope then staged on South Hampton Island, in upper Hudson Bay, for three weeks before leaving on a non-stop southern flight of more than 5,600 km (3,500 mi) over the open Atlantic Ocean to Great Pond on St. Croix Island in the U.S. Virgin Islands in the Caribbean Sea, where she spent the winter months. In less than one year, she traveled more than 29,000 km (18,000 mi)! [Ref 2-7]

Hope wintered on St. Croix for nearly eight months—from 14 August 2009, where she was observed foraging on Great Pond (a Birdlife International Important Bird Area) until leaving on the evening of 9 April 2010. She then flew east of Puerto Rico and northwest over the open Atlantic Ocean toward the U.S. East Coast for nearly 2,400 km (1,500 mi). She came near land around Cape Lookout, North Carolina and followed the shoreline around the Outer Banks of North Carolina and up to the lower Delmarva Peninsula, making landfall on 11 April 2010. The entire Atlantic trip covered about 2,678 km (1,660 mi) in less than two days. She settled on the same Virginia marsh where she had been captured by CCB biologists in the spring of 2009.

Hope then left her Virginia staging area on 22 May 2010 and flew for 12 days, covering 5,070 km (3,150 mi), to the Mackenzie River Delta, arriving on 4 June 2010, after having stopped briefly along the coast of Hudson Bay. She once again spent the summer in the Mackenzie Delta, likely incubating eggs while there. Hope then flew to Southampton Island, Hudson Bay, where she staged for the great flight down to her wintering grounds in the mangroves of Great Pond in the Caribbean.

While her satellite transmitter continued to work, researchers tracked Hope for more than 80,000 km (50,000 mi) traveling back and forth between her breeding area on the Mackenzie River in western Canada and her wintering site, at Great Pond on St. Croix. Her transmitter antenna shut off in early September 2012 shortly after she arrived on Great Pond. The Center for Conservation Biology then decided to remove the transmitter rather than replace it. She was captured on 20 November 2012 and her transmitter was removed. In subsequent years she would be identified by her coded leg flag (AYY). Hope returned to her wintering grounds, where she was recognized by her leg band, for five more seasons. [Ref 2-8]

On 26 August 2017 Hope was photographed by Lisa Yntema after arrival on her winter territory at Great Pond. On September 6, St. Croix was hit by Hurricane Irma as a category five storm experiencing heavy rain and structural damage. Following the storm, Lisa visited Great Pond and saw Hope on September 11. This was the last time that Lisa saw Hope.

Less than two weeks later, on September 19, St. Croix was hit by Hurricane Maria, with the eye wall passing directly over Great Pond. Lisa went to Great Pond on October 5 and found a single whimbrel on Hope's territory, but did not see Hope. Lisa visited Great Pond several more times through the fall of 2017 but did not find Hope. Barry Truitt, who was the chief conservation scientist for The Nature Conservancy's Virginia Coast reserve, also spent time searching for Hope within her spring staging area on Boxtree Creek in Virginia in April and May of 2018, but he did not find her. Hope did not return to Great Pond during the fall of 2018. [Ref 2-9]

Hope was immortalized in a children's book, *Hope is Here!* [Ref 2-10] She became an ambassador for shorebird migrants—and ultimately was the reason for the preservation and protection of Great Pond on St. Croix Island. [Ref 2-11]

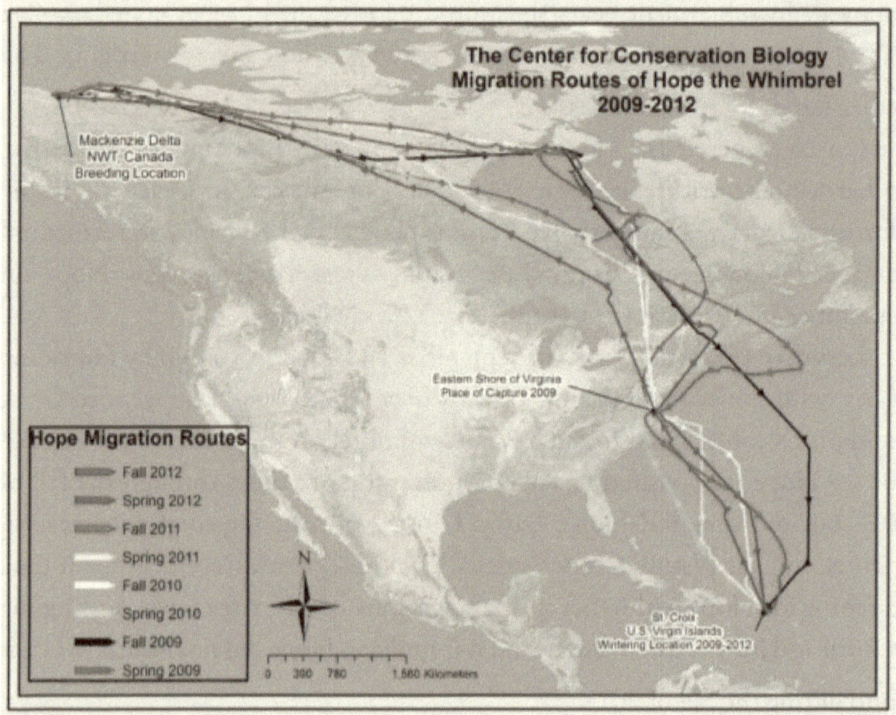

FIGURE 2-2 – MAP OF Hope's movements from the spring of 2009 to the fall of 2012 as tracked by satellite transmitter. Image Credit: Center for Conservation Biology at the College of William and Mary, Virginia Commonwealth University.

FIG 2-3 – PHOTO OF mangrove habitat within Hope's winter territory on St. Croix. Image Credit: Fletcher Smith, Center for Conservation Biology at the College of William and Mary, Virginia Commonwealth University.

FIG 2-4 – LISA YNTEMA with Hope after capture to remove transmitter in November of 2012. Image Credit: Fletcher Smith, Center for Conservation Biology at the College of William and Mary, Virginia Commonwealth University.

FIGURE 2-5 - HOPE ON 26 August 2017 after arriving at Great Pond. This photo was taken just two weeks before the arrival of Hurricane Irma. Photo by Lisa Yntema.

Hope's migratory feats are amazing. Whimbrels are not the only bird species who undertake these astounding migrations. Many species of birds are super-human athletes. Researchers are now using new and continually-developing technologies to track birds with radar and satellites using geolocators, and they are beginning to document the phenomenal migrations different birds make.

In North America, most bird species migrate to some extent, with more than 350 species travelling between their summer ranges in the United States and Canada, to more southerly locations to overwinter. Worldwide at least 4,000 bird species or about 40 percent of the total number of birds are regular migrants. (Ref 2-12)

Migration distances vary greatly between species as well as between individual birds of the same species. Some of the longest migrations are made by birds that nest in the Arctic tundra of northernmost Canada and winter as far south as the southernmost part of South America.

In the fall, up to 12 million migrants leave the coast of New England and embark on an 80 to 90 hour non-stop flight, traveling out past Bermuda and from there continuing to the coast of South America. For some tiny birds, like the Blackpoll Warbler, their migrations require a degree of exertion unmatched by any other vertebrate. It is the equivalent to a human's running a 4-minute mile for 80 hours. Blackpoll Warblers nearly double their weight from 11 to 21 grams before making their monumental journey.

The Arctic Tern holds the record for the longest migrations known in the animal kingdom. It nests as far north as there is land, on islands around the Arctic Sea. Then in early September it flies south offshore to the fringes of the Antarctic Ocean. Recent studies [Ref 2-13] have shown average Arctic Tern annual roundtrip lengths of about 70,900 km (44,100 mi) for birds nesting in Iceland and Greenland. The birds take meandering courses rather than following a straight route as was previously assumed. They follow a somewhat convoluted course in order to take advantage of prevailing winds. The average Arctic tern lives about thirty years, and will, based on the above research, travel some 2.4 million km (1.5 million mi) during its lifetime, the equivalent of a roundtrip from the Earth to the Moon over three times.

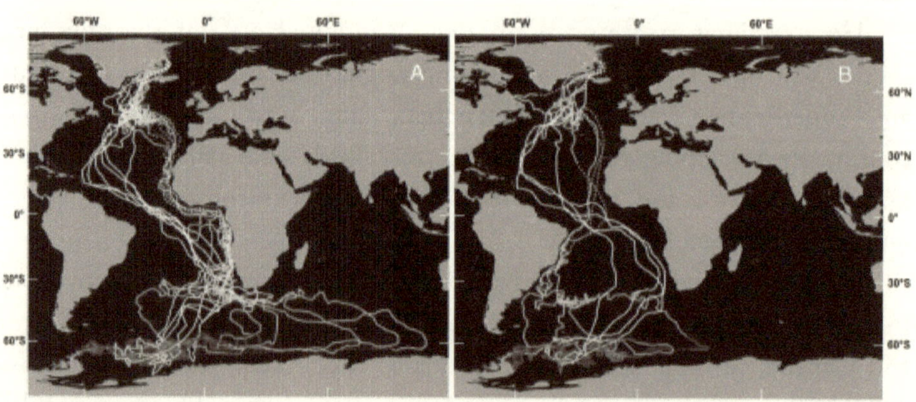

FIGURE 2-6 - INTERPOLATED geolocation tracks of 11 Arctic terns tracked from breeding colonies in Greenland (n = 10 birds) and Iceland (n = 1 bird). Two southbound migration routes were adopted in the South Atlantic, either (A) West African coast (n = 7 birds) or (B) Brazilian coast

https://www.pnas.org/content/107/5/2078

Summary of distances traveled during migration stages of Arctic terns (Greenland and Iceland birds combined, $n = 11$)

Migration segment	Distance traveled
Total distance traveled on migration	70,900 km (59,500–81,600 km)
Distance traveled on southbound migration	34,600 km (28,800–38,500 km)
Distance traveled per day on southbound migration	330 km·day^{-1} (280–390 km·day^{-1})
Distance traveled on northbound migration	25,700 km (21,400–34,900 km)
Distance traveled per day on northbound migration	520 km·day^{-1} (390–670 km·day^{-1})
Distance traveled within winter site	10,900 km (2,700–21,600 km)

WHY DO BIRDS MIGRATE? Migration has evolved as it is closely linked to encountering predictable seasonal opportunities, such as plenty of food for themselves and their offspring, reduced competition for territory, and lower predation risk.

Birds of northern regions migrate south because of sharp seasonal changes in climate—a secondary reason—and the resultant failure of their food supply—the primary reason. Temperature is almost never a primary factor with birds. Of all living creatures, birds are the most perfectly adapted to withstand extremes of temperatures. Most birds, if they get enough to eat, can survive the temperatures of a northern winter, whether they have ever previously experienced them or not. Human beings cannot compete with birds in their ability to withstand low temperatures. To think of birds as "delicate little creatures" is a delusion. They go south because the falling temperatures remove their food supply. [Ref 2-14]

The great majority of North American migrating birds winter in the tropics. For those birds that winter near the equator, there is no change in the length of daylight hours nor is there the slightest change in the average temperature throughout the year. What, then, starts these birds northward in mid-March? As these tropical wintering birds move northward, the average temperature is, for them, decreasing. Looking at the highly migratory North American shorebirds that breed in the Arctic and winter in southern South America, their situation becomes even more paradoxical, because they leave southern South America, northbound, in March and April. This is the middle of fall in south temperate climates, and the number of daylight hours and the temperate have been steadily decreasing for some time. Whatever impulse starts them on their journey to their breeding grounds, it is not any increase in temperature or in daylight hours. [Ref 2-15]

Birds undergo monumental migrations because these migrations, evolved over many generations, have proven favorable to the overall continuation of their species. These migrations may not be optimal for the individual bird of the species. Concerning the extraordinary and remarkable powers of bird flight demonstrated in shorebirds, the ornithologist Ludlow Griscom commented: "As far as our knowledge of these shorebirds is concerned, we have no clue as to the reason for their tremendous migration; we do not know what caused it, or whether it is of a necessity or advantage to the species biologically in modern times or not." [Ref 2-16]

The suggestion has been made that neotropical migrants may be returning to the general area of their ancestral home after breeding. The present northern breeding ranges may have been acquired as a means of overcoming the overwhelming competition and congestion in the tropics. Certain Arctic nesting shorebirds may be an illustration of this theory in the northern hemisphere. These birds are Arctic only in the sense that they nest north of the Arctic Circle. After breeding, they go south. For example, the Sanderling, although it nests only in the High Arctic, is found on nearly all temperate and tropical sandy beaches throughout the world. It has the greatest winter range of any bird in the New World. [Ref 2-17]

Dr. Henry Smith Williams held a theory concerning the origins of bird migration which he called the "emigration – migration formula". [Ref 2-18] This theory of migration hypothesizes that the migration routes of today duplicate the emigration routes of yesterday.

"A changed environment which alters the balance of nature so as to permit various species of birds to prosper, in turn forces the increasing population to find new feeding and breeding grounds. This is bird emigration. The new colonists, in migrating, follow back the known emigration route by which their recent ancestors invaded the regions of present habitat. They have no choice but to follow that instinct which impels them back along the series of homes of their forebearers that in aggregate make up the emigration route of the past – and the migration route of today. Birds no more decide where they shall go in winter than where they shall be born. The spell of their ancestors is their nemesis." [Ref 2-19]

Birds return to their same breeding grounds year after year and maintain their territories. However, young birds return, not to the exact place where they were born, but to the locations where they spent their adolescent days. By this process, the descendants of any pair of birds may spread in an ever-widening circle. Thus, the species as a whole emigrates, while every individual holds to the home-staying principle. This is the way that birds normally extend their breeding range. Each individual returns to an area close to where it was born to breed. If birds in general did not adhere to this "homing" principle, there would be "such chaos in the bird world as would obtain in a city where inhabitants should decide to pay no attention to their legal dwellings, but to seek shelter and food in whatever house was nearest or seemed most inviting." [Ref 2-20]

This law explains why birds on migration will pass over perfectly suitable breeding habitat, even if this habitat has no other competitors for its resources.

Albert Hochbaum [Ref 2-21] observed the same phenomenon with migrating ducks. He wrote about the "broken traditions" where birds were exterminated from a local area. He explained that once all the local breeders from an area were destroyed, there were none to return to these areas to breed. Historically, settlers may have thought there was no harm in taking a modest harvest of local birds every year, especially considering the flocks that passed through. However, in a few years, this predation gradually thinned local nesters down to a few widely-scattered birds. When the last families were taken, their traditions were dead. The lakes, with their "rushy borders and the muskrats upon whose houses these wildfowl nested, have survived to please the settlers' grandchildren, but the native geese and swans are gone".

By annually taking a few from the home marsh, eventually no local breeding birds were left. Although many ducks continued to pass by in spring migrations, few or none stopped to nest once the birds with the local breeding traditions were gone.

In *To Ride the Wind* Albert Hochbaum wrote [Ref 2-22]: "It is their destiny to ride the wind that carries them to faraway places. They leave at sundown, dark against the blaze, pursuing their course by measures man does not yet comprehend. This annual rhythm of travel has been the way of waterfowl from the beginning of their time, one hundred million years before Homo sapiens evolved as a human being."

"Birds inherit in their DNA the information they need to migrate in the right direction. They are also genetically programmed to fly a set distance. They use the same vector or dead-reckoning navigation program used by Charles Lindberg to fly from New York to Paris – i.e. travel steadily in a given compass direction for a predetermined time." [Ref 2-23]

But besides instinct, birds learn from experience. Solar orientation, stellar navigation, and magnetism are all part of a migrating bird's skill set. They can detect polarized light from sunlight's penetration through the atmosphere and researchers believe that the pattern of polarized light in the evening sky is the primary cue that provides a reference for a bird's orientation.

Land birds and waterfowl use the stars, especially constellations, as a source of directional information when navigating during migration. In addition to using the sun, stars, and landscapes, birds may actually be able to see the magnetic field of the earth. All these multiple sources of directional information form an intricate system of migration that enables them to migrate to and from the same breeding, wintering, and stopover locations year after year.

In the spring, migrating birds experience a change in their brain centers that controls hunger and feelings of fullness and, as a result, they gain weight by overeating. [Ref 2-24] When a bird isn't migrating, fat comprises about three to five percent of its body weight. Short- and middle-distance migrants increase their fat load to about 15% of their weight, while long-distance migrants increase their fat to 30 to 50% of their weight. They are literally obese. This fat fuels the aerobic contraction of flight muscles, allowing the birds to make long flights with minimal fatigue.

In the spring, many small birds leave South America from the tip of the Yucatan Peninsula and fly across the Gulf of Mexico, with some birds reaching the United States anywhere from western Louisiana to northwestern Florida. A passage of 500 to 700 miles (800 to 1,120 km) across the Gulf of Mexico is involved. This can be regarded as a very remarkable and extraordinary route, but millions of small land birds are able to do it twice each year. If they were not able to do it, they would long since have become extinct, or would have learned to go around either by the West Indies and Florida, or via Central America, Mexico and Texas.

Approximately two thirds of migratory songbirds in eastern North America negotiate the Gulf of Mexico. [Ref 2-25] A 2015 study tracked songbirds who fly across the Gulf of Mexico in fall migration. The study investigated the factors associated with birds' departure decisions, arrival at the Yucatan Peninsula, and crossing times. The findings suggest that a bird's fat reserves, as well as low humidity indicative of favorable weather patterns, shape departure decisions. Fat, date, and wind conditions predict whether birds will arrive in the Yucatan Peninsula. The study highlighted the complex decision-making process involved in crossing the Gulf.

Fat score was the primary factor related to the departure decision and successful crossing. Birds departing the northern Gulf coast with large fat reserves have a larger buffer for dealing with deteriorating weather conditions over open water. Thus birds can exert some control over their ability to mitigate the risk of crossing the Gulf by increasing their fat reserves before departure, providing they can locate and acquire food resources. The study's findings emphasize the value of high-quality habitat along the edge of geographic features that offer few, if any, refueling opportunities. In coastal areas, where human impacts are high, foraging opportunities may be reduced, thus limiting birds' ability to gain sufficient fat for nonstop flights over water.

The study found that age appeared unrelated to a successful crossing of the Gulf. [Ref 2-26] Provided young birds had sufficient fat and departed over water under favorable conditions, their likelihood of arrival at the Yucatan Peninsula, crossing times, and cross-Gulf flight durations were undistinguishable from those of adult birds, demonstrating that they are able to manage the risks associated with the Gulf of Mexico the first time they encounter it.

The study made the following observations: [Ref 2-27] "Accounts of thousands of songbirds washing ashore, exhausted songbirds alighting on offshore structures or boats, terrestrial birds in the stomachs of sharks, and flights away from the coast in seasonally inappropriate directions reinforce the view that crossing the Gulf of Mexico presents considerable risk. However, though the Gulf is often considered a barrier, large numbers of birds routinely cross it and arrive on the opposite coast in good energetic condition, suggesting that the Gulf is not inherently a barrier. Rather, the risks of the crossing and the extent to which the Gulf functions as a barrier appear to be determined by weather and fat reserves. By coordinating the timing and orientation of departure with favorable conditions, crossing large bodies of open water can be quick, energy efficient, and safe. Under such conditions, crossing features like the Gulf should be preferred to circumnavigating them, because crossing can substantially reduce travel distances and time while reducing exposure to predators and pathogens."

A 2018 study published in Proceedings of the Royal Society B [Ref 2-28] provided the first survival estimates for small migratory birds crossing the Gulf: "Survival estimates varied with wind profit and fat, but generally, fat birds departing on days with favorable wind profits had an apparent survival probability of greater than 0.90, while lean individuals with no or negative wind profits had less than 0.33."

Mike Ward, who is an associate professor in the Department of Natural Resources and Environmental Sciences at the University of Illinois, and avian ecologist at the Illinois Natural History Survey, commented regarding the decision that birds make when determining whether or not to start a flight across the Gulf: [Ref 2-29]

"Birds that aren't fat enough know it. When they fly up in the sky at dusk, they circle around a little bit and head back north to find more food. The really fat ones – we call them little butterballs – fly up in the sky then start heading south. As long as they don't have a strong wind in their face, they should be fine. Individuals with intermediate levels of fat have to make a tough decision."

Ward says [Ref 2-30] that from a conservation perspective there's not much people can do to control the wind, but conservation efforts can improve birds' chances of surviving the journey across the Gulf. People can help the birds to get fat before making the crossing.

"If people throughout the migration corridor provide habitat and food sources for birds to add fat, they're facilitating their ability to cross the Gulf even if the winds aren't ideal. Whether it's planting native shrubs in your backyard, or setting aside a big tract of forest, I'm a big proponent that every small thing helps."

The Texas Parks & Wildlife Department publishes a list of the following bird species who cross the Gulf of Mexico from the Yucatan Peninsula to the United States Gulf Coast from Texas to Florida. They note that trans-Gulf migration is characteristic of these species, but does not exclude the possibility of some birds going around the Gulf of Mexico. Bird migration is subject to variation among individual birds. In the biological world there are rules, but there are always exceptions. [Ref 2-31]

Chimney Swift, Ruby-throated Hummingbird, Belted Kingfisher, Yellow-bellied Sapsucker, Black-billed Cuckoo, Yellow-billed Cuckoo, Common Nighthawk, Chuck-will's-widow, Whip-poor-will, Olive-sided Flycatcher, Eastern Wood-Pewee, Eastern Phoebe, Great Crested Flycatcher, Eastern Kingbird, Western Kingbird, Scissor-tailed Flycatcher, White-eyed Vireo, Blue-headed Vireo, Yellow-throated Vireo, Warbling Vireo, Philadelphia Vireo, Red-eyed Vireo, Purple Martin, Barn Swallow, Cliff Swallow, House Wren, Marsh Wren, Veery, Gray-cheeked Thrush, Swainson's Thrush, Scarlet Tanager, Hermit Thrush, Wood Thrush, Gray Catbird, Cedar Waxwing, Blue-winged Warbler, Golden-winged Warbler, Tennessee Warbler, Nashville Warbler, Northern Parula, Yellow Warbler, Chestnut-sided Warbler, Magnolia Warbler, Cape May Warbler, Black-throated Blue Warbler, Blackburnian Warbler, Yellow-throated Warbler, Prairie Warbler, Palm Warbler, Bay-breasted Warbler, Blackpoll Warbler, Cerulean Warbler, Black-and-White Warbler, American Redstart, Prothonotary Warbler, Worm-eating Warbler, Swainson's Warbler,

Ovenbird, Northern Waterthrush, Louisiana Waterthrush, Kentucky Warbler, Common Yellowthroat, Hooded Warbler, Yellow-breasted Chat, Summer Tanager, Scarlet Tanager, Rose-breasted Grosbeak, Blue Grosbeak, Dickcissel, Bobolink, Orchard Oriole, Baltimore Oriole

Many dangers threaten the birds during migration, including storms, predators, and the disappearance of their usual stopover places where they are accustomed to finding rest and food. Dr. Henry Smith Williams commented: "The Gulf is the grave of millions of migrants each season. And there are minor hazards along the whole 3,000-mile migration route. We can never hope that even a majority of the summer residents that leave us in the autumn will return to us in the spring." He documented the return of Orchard Orioles to his Connecticut home as follows: [Ref 2-32]

1930 – 11 orioles' nests at colony

1931 – 5 orioles' nests at colony

1932 – 2 orioles' nests at colony

1933 – 2 orioles' nests at colony

1934 – only one male and no female returned

1936 – male returned for a fifth time

Dr. Henry Smith Williams has an answer to the question: Why did the birds' ancestors select the hazardous routes across the Gulf of Mexico now followed instinctively by their descendants? [Ref 2-33]

"The remote ancestors did not select routes that were ultra-hazardous. When (in a long, long series of generations) they first traversed the territory of the present migration trails, there were no long stretches of water to be crossed. There was ample land connection between the northern and southern continents, affording suitable feeding and breeding grounds for the ancestral birds, who were not at first migrating, in the modern sense of the word, but merely extending their habitat year by year or century by century, to meet the needs of increasing populations.

By such slow expansion, a species would extend its habitat, inch by inch as it were, until it compassed the zones, as far as climatic conditions permitted. Ultimately regions were reached where life could not be maintained throughout the year; and from such regions the birds must retire—back along the ancestral emigration route—for the winter. Every inch of this route was originally favorable terrain for food and shelter. If more recent geologic changes made life no longer tenable in some areas, the wings of the birds make it possible to pass over these and complete the journey to the safe haven of the original habitat. The migration trail of any bird today is the emigration trail or route of its long series of remote ancestors. There is no other plausible theory to explain the diversity of migration routes as observed today."

Birds are capable of making some adjustments in their migrations. It has been shown that conditions on migratory routes influence the migratory speed for some birds. Temperature on migration plays an increasingly important role in driving the arrival time on their breeding grounds for these birds. [Ref 2-34] For some high latitude populations, the speed of migration appears to be the main determinant of the timing of arrival on the breeding grounds, rather than the timing of departure from the wintering grounds. If birds encounter colder than normal conditions as they fly north, they may slow down their migration.

"Studies of the Yellow Warbler (*Dendroica petechia*) indicate that the timings of arrival and clutch initiation in a population breeding in southern Manitoba, Canada, are strongly correlated with the degree of spring warming, with little impact of the weather conditions on the wintering grounds." [Ref 2-35]

In the spring, migrating pink-footed geese time their movements according to temperature to ensure there is sufficient grass for them to eat. The growth of grass, which is their main food in the spring, is temperature-related. Geese can track variation between years in the rate of improvement in feeding conditions at different stopover sites. The influence that conditions on the wintering grounds have on arrival time at the breeding grounds declines with increasing migratory distance.

Trends in migrant arrival for some European species, particularly of short- and medium-distance migrants, can be explained by large-scale climatic indices, such as the North Atlantic Oscillation (NAO). These effects are likely to result from positive-phase NAO being indicative of warm weather on the wintering grounds. The NAO is in a positive phase when both the sub-polar low and the subtropical high are stronger than average. During positive NAO phases, the increased difference in pressure between the two regions results in a stronger

Atlantic jet stream and a northward shift of the storm track. Consequently, northern Europe experiences increased storminess and precipitation, and warmer-than-average temperatures associated with the air masses that arrive from lower latitudes.

Humans have caused many changes to the environment that are difficult for birds to respond and adapt to. There are six components of global change—habitat alteration, climate change, chemical inputs, over-exploitation of natural resources, and biological invasions. Threats from habitat alteration and loss are compounded by climate change, which causes increasing carbon dioxide concentrations, warmer temperatures, rising global sea level, melting polar ice packs, expanding drylands and deserts, and an increase in extreme weather events such as heat waves, floods, storms, and cyclones. Current climate change effects are happening very quickly, making it very difficult for birds to respond to these changes.

Long-distance migrants are at a disadvantage to short-distance migrants and to resident birds in their ability to adapt to the unpredictable changes caused by human development and climate change. They have acquired many physical and cognitive adaptations over many generations which are embedded deep in their genes. They are perhaps the most susceptible to unpredictable changes that occur in their environments. [Ref 2-36] It would be difficult for them to be able to adapt quickly enough to rapid changes in their environment.

Long-distant migrants often have inborn programs guiding them about the onset, duration, and direction of migration. Many long-distance migrant birds show adaptations of various types– including longer wings, migratory fattening, and nocturnal restlessness prior to migration. They are characterized by having a long-term memory which allows them to remember high-quality stopover sites, prior year breeding territories, and former winter locations. They are not as curious to investigate the environments they inhabit. Migrants who rely largely on memory, who explore little, and who have low flexibility to respond to unpredictable environmental change, currently often show declining population trends.

Migratory species often return to the same breeding and wintering grounds year after year. While this is an advantage in a predictable environment, it can be disadvantageous when conditions change. Stopover and breeding sites may have shifted, changed, or disappeared. Site fidelity can be either less productive if the birds now return to a less satisfactory site, or in the worst case, can mean death when habitats become unsuitable.

The Arctic is experiencing warming from climate change at twice the rate of the rest of the world. The Arctic habitat is shrinking from year to year, accompanied by the melting of permafrost, the northerly rise of shrubs and sub-forests, and the narrowing of tundra habitats. In response to climate warming, the extension of forested formations in latitude and altitude results in a shrinkage, estimated at 40 to 57 percent by the end of the 21st century, of habitats essential to many goose and shorebird species.

As long-distance migrants, it is important that shorebirds find suitable habitat in their breeding, migration, and winter habitats. Any break in the chain puts these birds at risk. Of 49 North American shorebird species recently assessed, 90 percent were predicted to have an increased risk of extinction due to climate change alone. [Ref 2-37] Conservation efforts should particularly address habitats used by long-distance migrants as they have the largest problems coping with change. Conservation efforts require maintaining suitable, non-disturbed (or only slightly disturbed) habitats on the breeding and overwintering ground, and at migration stopover sites.

Although birds can make some adaptations to help them when their environment changes, they are still dependent on requirements essential to their survival, such as obtaining adequate food. They can fly and are mobile, but if there is no suitable environment within their flying range, they cannot survive.

The northward and southward limits of birds in North America are highly complex and elaborate combinations of factors, such as past history; the accident of survival; humidity; and the presence or absence of favorable habitat requirements. [Ref 2-38]

Currently, the effects of climate change are severely impacting the lives of many sea and coastal birds due to factors such as sea-level rise, ocean acidification, and altered food supplies. All 67 ocean bird species in United States waters, such as petrels, albatross, and murres, are considered at medium or high vulnerability, making them one of the most at-risk group of United States birds due to climate change. [Ref 2-39]

In 1945, the ornithologist Ludlow Griscom wrote: "In my lifetime, various birds have been steadily pushing northward and northeastward, and it follows that the present isothermal lines of their northernmost limits are very much cooler than those that constituted their northern limits 25 years ago. Temperature has not limited the northward distribution of these birds......However, the White Pelican winters in numbers on the Gulf Coast of Texas and practically every summer a certain number of White Pelicans used to linger on their southern wintering grounds. They attempted to breed; they laid eggs; and the eggs hatched. But the young fried to death in the blazing heat of the Texas beaches in the May and June sun. It was some years before any White Pelican succeeded in raising a young bird to maturity in the southern Texas area, and the extreme heat of the summer climate there is a limiting factor." [Ref 2-40]

As the ocean heats, it can have dramatic impacts on the biological timing of microscopic species, which are the base of the food chain. This impacts the fish, some of which die or move north in search of colder water. In turn, the sea birds, seals, walrus, and other species that feed on the fish are negatively impacted.

Researchers estimate an unprecedented 500,000 to one million Common Murres died along the Pacific Coast during an ocean heat wave which occurred in 2014 through 2016. In a study published in January 2020 in the journal *PLOS ONE*, a group of scientists from various state and federal agencies, universities, and bird rescue organizations documented the die-off and concluded from the data that it was caused by this record-breaking ocean heat wave that triggered systemic changes throughout the ocean ecosystem.

The ocean heat wave was a result of the coming together of several causal factors at the same time—(1) the ocean's getting warmer due to global warming; (2) the Pacific Decadal Oscillation—a recurring pattern of ocean-atmospheric climate variability that leads to periods of warming in the mid-latitude Pacific; (3) a strong El Niño event from 2015-2016 which led to warming from California's coast up to Alaska; and (4) a ridge of high pressure over land on the Northwest coast of North America that blocked airflow from the Pacific Ocean to the interior, trapping heat over the ocean. [Ref 2-41]

A marine heat wave is defined as a coherent area of extremely warm sea surface temperature that persists for days to months. Recent marine heat waves have caused devastating impacts on marine ecosystems. Substantial progress in understanding past and future changes in marine heat waves and their risks for marine ecosystems is needed to predict how marine systems, and the goods and services they provide, will evolve in the future. (Ref 2-42)

Thomas Frölicher, a climate scientist at the University of Bern in Switzerland commented about the northeast Pacific marine heatwave of 2014-16 as follows: "It was the biggest marine heat wave so far on record...Usually, we are used to heat waves over land. They are much smaller in size, and they do not last as long. In the ocean, this heat wave lasted two or three years." (Ref 2-43)

In the past 35 years, marine heat waves have doubled in frequency, Frölicher said. And as global temperatures continue to rise, they will become even more commonplace. "If we follow a high-greenhouse-gas-emissions scenario, these heat waves will become 50 times more frequent than in preindustrial times" by the year 2100. A low-emissions scenario, consistent with the Paris climate agreement, would still see 20 times more heat waves. "What that means is that in some regions, they will become permanent heat waves," he said. The mass deaths of Common Murres suggests what that may look like. "This gives us some insight into the future." (Ref 2-44)

Huge variations in migratory practices have occurred repeatedly in the history of birds, especially during the Pleistocene period 2.6 million to 11,700 years ago, with its alternating glacial and interglacial periods. Under current pressures, many migratory species will have to modify their migratory behavior if they are to meet the new challenges caused by the deterioration of conditions along their established migration routes. Individuals of a given species often differ considerably from each other in their response to environmental challenges—termed personality—which on the population level increases flexibility and adaptability.

David Attenborough in *The Life of Birds* commented: "And the shape of birds to come? That can only be guessed at, as birds continue to adapt to habitats and changing conditions. One thing is certain. Such a versatile creature will always be with us, and with our distant descendants." [Ref 2-45]

Dr. Henry Smith Williams commented on seeing migrant birds returning to their summer home: [Ref 2-46] "Well may we wonder, then, at the dauntless courage, the amazing adaptiveness, the strength of wing and the tireless energy of the band of survivors that come home to us each season. Theirs is the triumph of audacity against overwhelming odds. We love them for their beauty of form and color, for their delightful personalities, and for the dangers they have passed."

Chapter 3 – Be Vigilant and Aware of Your Surroundings

"Awareness is the first step to action. They have to know something is going on to know to do something about it."

Derick Virgil

"Awareness requires living in the here and now, and not in the elsewhere, the past or the future."

Eric Berne

"Awareness is becoming acquainted with the environments, no matter where one happens to be."

Sigurd F. Olson

"As I stood above the burdens that puzzle you and me, I became awareness that was shared with all around, with the trees, the sky, the flowers, and the wind, the sun, the ground."

Derroll Adams

Birds are aware of their surroundings. They need to be vigilant about potential dangers in their environment and to watch for predators.

An example of constant alertness is seen in birds sitting on a beach who all face in the same direction. No matter how many gulls, terns, pelicans, or shore birds are gathered on a beach, they will face into the wind. If anything disturbs a flock of birds facing into the wind, it will lift them effortlessly off the sand when they open their wings. Birds have more control over their movements if they lift off into the wind. Control is more difficult going with the wind, especially a strong wind. If they rest with tails to the wind, their feathers become twisted in all directions, making for a very uncomfortable and nonflight-ready condition. (Ref 3-1)

FIGURE 3-1 – RUDDY Turnstones on Beach facing in the same direction into the wind. Image by Pixsas from Pixabay.

The author often observed a Long-billed Curlew at Crissy Field Marsh on San Francisco's northern waterfront. The curlew was always aware of her surroundings, and of the author's watching her.

The Long-billed Curlew

Very few people pay any attention to the birds in Crissy Field Marsh on San Francisco's northern waterfront. The Golden Gate Promenade beside the marsh is often crowded with people walking, jogging and bicycling. Only a low wire fence separates the marsh from the Golden Gate Promenade walkway, but people stay on the path and do not even look out at the marsh to see the birds. No-one bothers the birds, and the always-watchful birds are comfortable going about their business in the marsh.

Over a period of several years, I regularly saw a Long-billed Curlew with a very long bill in Crissy Field Marsh. Because of her extremely long bill, she was a female. She seemed to own the far eastern side of the marsh and always inhabited this part of the marsh. There were areas of cinnamon among her black/gray/brown/buff body and when she lifted up a wing, she had pure cinnamon-colored wing linings. She was a gorgeous bird, and I loved to watch her.

Over a period of several winters, I was privileged to watch this bird feeding, preening, resting and interacting with other birds in the marsh. The curlew was aware of my standing by the side of the path watching her and taking pictures of her, but she continued going about her business. She often looked straight at me and sometimes walked towards me.

At 7:00 p.m. on May 11, 2018 the water level was low in the marsh with much land showing above the water line. I saw the curlew walking along the edge of the water quite far away and I watched her through binoculars. Suddenly, she stopped walking and stood very still, looking at something. A large dark raptor-type bird had landed on the ground a short distance away from her. The curlew did not move and kept looking at this potential predator. Finally, the raptor took off, flying west over to the far side of the marsh. Both the curlew and I watched as it flew over the edge of the marsh. We saw it swoop down and heard a small Killdeer cry out. I could not see what had happened and hoped the Killdeer had been able to escape the raptor. After a while, the curlew began walking again.

The curlew was so aware of her surroundings. She immediately noticed the raptor even though she was also concentrating on trying to find something to eat.

A study showed that birds overcome the problem of sleeping in risky situations by developing the ability to sleep with one eye open and one hemisphere of the brain awake. [Ref 3-2] Birds that are literally half-asleep—with one brain hemisphere alert and the other snoozing—control which side of the brain remains awake. The brain hemispheres take turns sinking into the sleep stage characterized by slow brain waves. The eye controlled by the sleeping hemisphere shuts, while the wakeful hemisphere's eye stays open and vigilant. Birds also can sleep with both hemispheres resting at once.

To check whether birds can control half-brain sleeping, the study looked at rows of Mallards napping. Decades of studies of bird flocks had led researchers to predict extra vigilance in the more vulnerable, end-of-the-row sleepers. Sure enough, the end birds tended to keep open the eye on the side facing away from their buddies. Mallards snuggled into the inner spots showed no preference for gaze direction. Also, birds dozing at the end of the line resorted to single-hemisphere sleep, rather than total relaxation, more often than inner ducks did. Rotating 16 birds through the positions in a four-duck row, the researchers found outer birds half-asleep during some 32% of snoozing time versus about 12% for birds in internal spots.

"We believe this is the first evidence for an animal behaviorally controlling sleep and wakefulness simultaneously in different regions of the brain," the researchers said. The results provided the best evidence yet for a long-standing conjecture that single- hemisphere sleep evolved as creatures scanned for predators. The preference for opening an eye on the lookout side could be widespread. Useful as half-sleeping might be, it's only been found in birds and such aquatic mammals as dolphins, whales, seals, and manatees. Presumably, keeping one side of the brain awake allows a submerged sleeping animal to surface occasionally to avoid drowning, explained Niels Rattenborg, the main author of the study. [Ref 3-3]

The author often watched a Long-billed Curlew and a Willet resting while at the same time keeping vigilant:

Watching Each Other's Back

In late fall and early winter, I often saw two large shorebirds feeding in the same area at the restored Crissy Field Marsh. One, a non-breeding Western Willet, was very plain gray. The other, larger one with very different coloring, had a buff and cinnamon underbody with a brown mottled head and back, and a very long downward-curving bill almost as long as its body. It was a Long-billed Curlew. These two birds spent their non-breeding time together at Crissy Field Marsh. They seemed to be friends. They both noticed me as I stood at the edge of the path watching them, but they did not seem disturbed by my presence and they came to know me.

On December 30, 2014 strong winds blew trees down in San Francisco and the streets were littered with debris from fallen tree branches. That night the wind howled and the following morning was still exceptionally windy from the northeast. Going out to Crissy Field Marsh, I noticed the white-capped waves in San Francisco Bay. At the marsh the water level was high. The Long-billed Curlew and Willet were on the bank at the side of the marsh. They were six inches apart and were resting together on the south side of this ridge, as much out of the wind as possible.

The curlew had her long bill tucked under her scapulars and was standing on one leg. She had one eye open, observing her surroundings. Meanwhile, the willet stood almost back-to-back with her, and was turned the other way. The willet also had one eye open, monitoring in the opposite direction. What they were doing was like having eyes all around them. In this way, together the two birds could watch their environment from all directions. They were covering each other's backs. What intelligent birds! No wonder they got along so well together.

FIGURE 3-2 – WESTERN Willet in Crissy Field Marsh. Photo by the author.

FIGURE 3-3 – WESTERN Willet in breeding plumage at Crissy Field Marsh. Photo by the author.

FIGURE 3-4 - LONG-BILLED Curlew at Crissy Field Marsh. Photo by the author.

FIGURE 3-5 - LONG-BILLED Curlew and Western Willet resting together at the edge of Crissy Field Marsh. Photo by the author.

Chapter 4 –Value Cleanliness and Beauty

"Better keep yourself clean and bright; you are the window through which you must see the world."

George Bernard Shaw

"Cleanliness has a powerful influence on the health and preservation of the body."

W. Aspinwall

"A thing of beauty is a joy forever; its loveliness increases, it will never pass into nothingness."

John Keats

"Let us live for the beauty of our own reality."

Charles Lamb

"Neatness and cleanliness is not a function of how rich or poor you are but that of mentality and principle."

Ikechukwu Izuakor

Cleanliness is extremely important to birds. They spend hours every day maintaining their feathers by preening them. Clean feathers provide insulation and waterproofing, and enable aerodynamic flight. They are critical to a bird's survival and need to be constantly kept in good condition. Careful preening allows a bird to look its healthiest and most beautiful. A healthier, more attractive bird will attract a stronger mate and have a better chance to raise strong, healthy offspring. By preening and keeping their feathers in good order, birds accentuate their natural-born beauty.

Feathers are unique to birds and their dinosaur ancestors. They have evolved into impressive biological structures that come in a diversity of colors and forms. No bird is without feathers. Unlike mammals whose hair sprouts uniformly from the skin, most birds' feathers sprout in tracts with bare patches of skin between them. The birds' bare skin does not show because their feathers fan out to cover their bodies.

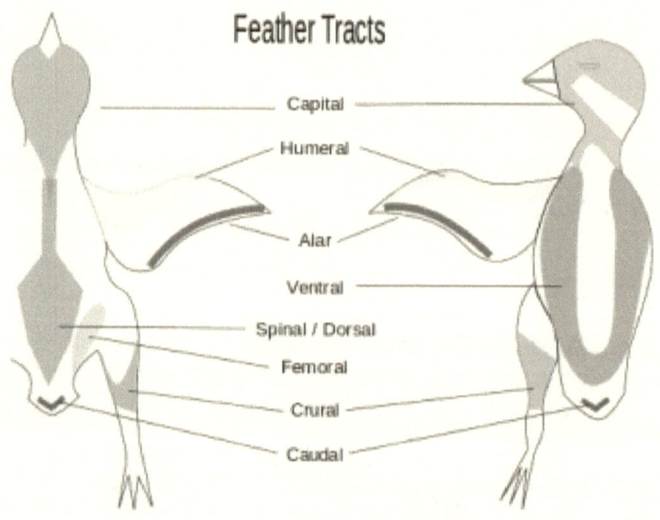

FIGURE 4-1 - PTERYLOSIS or feather tracts of a bird. Courtesy of L. Shyamal Shyamal, CC BY SA 3.0, via Wikimedia Commons.

Feathers are lightweight and strong and are the defining characteristic of birds. There are different categories of feathers which serve different functions. Flight contour feathers have a central shaft and countless barbs that protrude from either side, forming vanes. Contour feathers need to be both rigid and flexible. Strong, rigid vanes are especially important for flight. The central shaft provides structural support, while each barb of the feather has smaller barbs, or "barbules" which project from either side toward the adjacent barbs. The barbules on one side of the barb are straight, while those on the other are hooked. The barbules of adjacent barbs overlap, so the hooked barbules attach to the straight barbules of the other, making the vane rigid. If barbs separate and the vane splits, the bird can repair it by preening. Running the barbs through its bill reconnects the hooks like a zipper. (Ref 4-1)

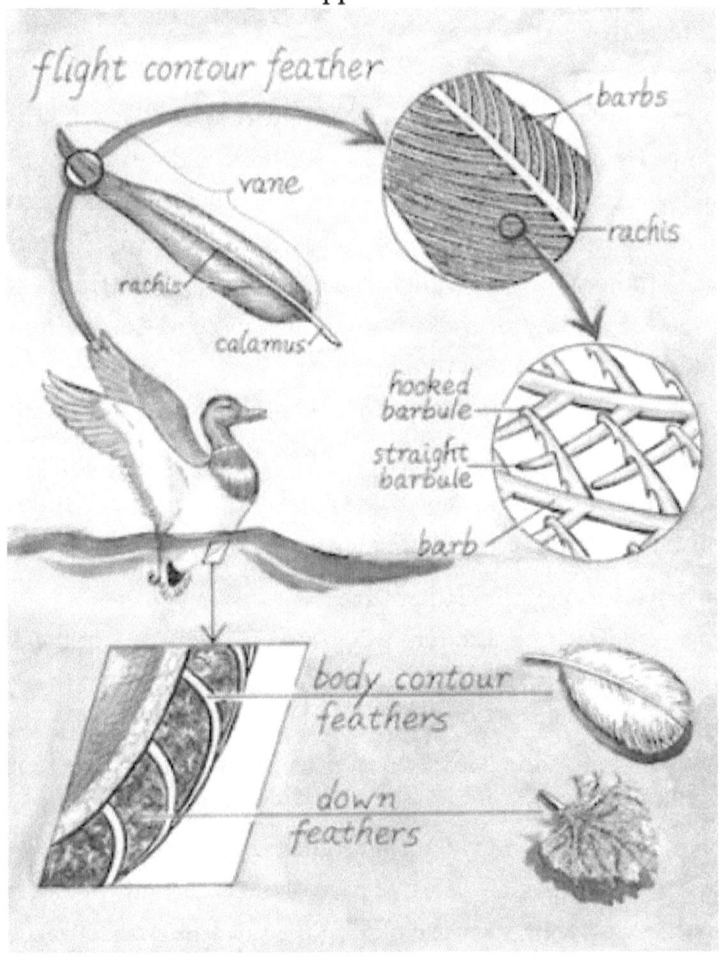

FIGURE 4-2 - OVERLAPPING barbules give contour feathers rigidity. Fluffy down feathers lack a rachis. Illustration by Denise Takahashi. *https://www.birdwatchingdaily.com/news/science/bird-basics-six-different-feather-types-explained/*

Smaller contour feathers cover the body and leading edges of the wings. On the wings, the feathers help form the airfoil shape that is necessary for flight. On the body, they contribute color, which is important in courtship and for camouflage, and they form a sleek outer covering, providing an aerodynamic tear-drop shape that assists flight. [Ref 4-2]

Short, loose, fluffy down feathers lie under the body's contour feathers, forming a mass of feathers that trap air and provide insulation. Birds can fluff up their down feathers to keep themselves warm in cold weather.

The number of feathers on a bird varies according to the species, the bird's age, and the season. Most small songbirds have between 1,500 and 3,000 feathers on their bodies. A swan might have as many as 25,000 feathers. Regular preening keeps each one of those feathers in top condition. Second only to feeding, preening is a common bird behavior.

Displaced feathers can interrupt the smooth flow of air over a flying bird, or allow the bird's body heat to escape. [Ref 4-3] Preening allows a bird to reposition such displaced feathers. Birds fluff up their plumage and repeatedly shake their bodies while preening. Experiments show that the shaking action can "rezip" a majority of split feather barbules. [Ref 4-4]

When a bird preens, it also removes any dirt, and picks out parasites from its plumage. During molt, birds remove the sheaths from around their emerging pin feathers while preening.

Preening is often done before or after other maintenance behaviors, such as bathing, dusting, sunning, or anting. All birds typically preen after bathing. Groups of birds often all individually groom at the same time.

The preen or uropygial gland is part of the preening process for most birds. This gland is found near the base of the tail and produces an oily, waxy substance. Birds use their beaks to distribute this oil over their feathers to help waterproof their feathers and keep them flexible. Some bird species—such as owls, Great Blue Herons, pigeons, and woodpeckers (who are less likely to immerse themselves in water), have powder down feathers that shed a very fine, white, waxy powder that is spread through the feathers when the bird preens.

For birds that live in the water, their feathers must provide them with an absolutely waterproof coat, or the cold water will reach their skin, causing them to suffer and die from hypothermia.

Oil spills are disastrous for birds. They ingest harmful or fatal amounts of oil during their frantic attempts to preen their feathers. When oil sticks to a bird's feathers, it causes the feathers to mat and separate, impairing waterproofing and exposing the animal's sensitive skin to extremes in temperature. This can result in hypothermia when the bird becomes cold, or hyperthermia when the bird overheats. Instinctively, the bird tries to get the oil off its feathers by preening, which results in the bird's ingesting the oil and causing severe damage to its internal organs. In this emergency situation, the focus on preening overrides all other natural behaviors, including evading predators and feeding, making the bird vulnerable to secondary health problems such as severe weight loss, anemia and dehydration. Many oil-soaked birds lose their buoyancy and beach themselves in their attempt to escape the cold water. The fortunate ones are captured by wildlife rescue crews and taken to rehabilitation centers where they are treated and given a chance to survive. (Ref 4-5)

As well as feathers, beaks require upkeep. After eating, birds carefully clean their beaks by swiping them from side to side against something hard. This also helps to wear down new beak growth and even out any chips or tiny breaks.

Feathers may serve as camouflage that protects birds against predators. Meadowlarks have a distinctive yellow throat and belly with a black "V" on the breast. However, when they turn to the back, their pale gray/brown mottled coloring blends in well with the grassy fields they inhabit.

FIGURE 4-3 – MEADOWLARK. Courtesy of Daniel Roberts from Pixabay.

The dangerously conspicuous appearance of many birds, especially the males, can only be explained on the grounds that the females of their species love bright colors, and persistently discriminate in favor of males that are most vividly feathered. "Birds and butterflies are lovers of beautiful colors; else they would not have come, through mating selection, to wear them." (Ref 4-6)

Birds' love of beauty has also influenced the vegetable world. The bright colors of flowers would not have developed were they not attractive to bees, butterflies, and hummingbirds. Wind-fertilized plants have neither sweet-scented nor conspicuously-colored flowers. (Ref 4-7)

The colors that humans see in birds' feathers are the result of pigments in the feathers. A pigment is a substance that appears a certain color because it selectively absorbs different wavelengths of light.

"You would never think of describing a Chipping Sparrow, a wren, or a Wood Thrush as a red and black bird. However, their feathers, as well as the feathers of every other brown-coated bird, owe their color to the blending of pigments that are red and black. There are no brown pigments in bird feathers.

Nature gets all her warm-tone effects by mixing pigment granules that are either black, red, or yellow. Many common birds have patches of red or yellow, which are more or less hidden, as adornments in their generally dull-toned plumage.

Blue and green feathers owe their color, not to pigment, but to certain physical characteristics of the surface, which result in breaking up of the light waves in such a way as to present to the human eye in greatest profusion the waves that are registered as blue or green. Blue pigment is entirely unknown in the plumage of any bird. Similarly, white is an optical illusion, and is due to the presence of air bubbles, as in snow crystals, and not to a pigment. White is almost universal as a variant or adornment of bird plumages of every color." (Ref 4-8)

FIGURE 4-4 – CALIFORNIA Scrub-Jay. Courtesy of Rick Brown from Pixabay.

How do the birds themselves see each other? "Nearly all birds see at least two or three times as much detail as humans, making them able to spot food – or approaching predators – that much farther away. Most birds have excellent color vision as well.

Another advantage birds have is seeing ultraviolet light. To humans, male and female Northern Mockingbirds look exactly the same – but birds are able to tell the difference because the two have different ultraviolet markings." [Ref 4-9]

Ultraviolet light is the name given to electromagnetic radiation with wavelengths between those of visible light and X-rays. It comes after "violet" in the spectrum. Scientists have known for decades that birds can see ultraviolet light because their eyes have an extra type of cone cell specifically tuned to detect those wavelengths. With ultraviolet vision, birds see a much different world than we do. Feather patches that to us seem unremarkable, shine brightly when viewed with ultraviolet vision. Many species of birds have plumage patterns that are only discernible in UV light. Species in which male and female birds appear identical to us have UV reflective patches on their feathers that enable the birds themselves to tell the sexes apart.

Birds are not alone in possessing ultraviolet (UV) vision. Certain animals like reindeer, sockeye salmon and butterflies have additional cones that enable them to perceive UV light.

Ultraviolet vision may enable birds to find certain fruits and berries. Some fruits and berries have waxy coatings that reflect UV light and stand out against green foliage, allowing birds to see them more easily. Some flowers and insects also reflect UV light giving birds an advantage for finding those food sources. (Ref 4-10)

Except for night-flying birds such as owls, the eyes of most birds probably are even more sensitive to UV light than they are to what humans call visible light. [Ref 4-11] Drake University biologist Muir Eaton commented: [Ref 4-12] "If you assume birds see exactly what we see, you could have the wrong framework for understanding bird behavior."

The increased availability and decreased cost of a laboratory device called the spectrophotometer—which precisely measures light reflected or absorbed by a surface—let scientists, if not see like a bird, at least quantify what birds are seeing.

In 2005, Eaton used a spectrophotometer to scan the plumage of museum study skins of 139 songbird species in which males and females appear alike, from Cedar Waxwings to Barn Swallows to Mockingbirds to Western Meadowlarks. Though scientists previously had classified these birds as sexually monochromatic (males and females looking identical), a full 90 percent of the species Eaton scanned were sexually dichromatic. They looked different once you took into account the better discrimination of colors (including UV) by birds and the amount of UV light the feathers reflect. "To the birds themselves, males and females look quite different from one another," said Eaton. [Ref 4-13]

Once formed, feathers are dead structures that cannot repair themselves when damaged. Feathers wear out from physical abrasion and bleaching from the sun and birds must molt to survive. Because a healthy and functional coat is critical to survival, each year birds shed their old feathers and then grow a whole new set. This molting process is a carefully timed affair in which feathers are shed and regenerate in turn over a period of weeks. Once a year (in the late summer for temperate species) birds grow an entirely new set of feathers through a complete molt. Some birds go through molt on or near their breeding grounds and migrate south after they have acquired a new set of feathers. Others start their migrations and then fly to an intermediate location to undergo their molt.

When birds grow new flight feathers, they are particularly vulnerable to predators. During wing molt, several of their flight feathers will be less than full length, producing gaps in their wings that render them less maneuverable and powerful in flight. To avoid attracting the attention of predators many birds—such as sparrows, warblers, and thrushes—lie low, calling infrequently and hiding in vegetation. [Ref 4-14]

Molt is extremely variable. Observed patterns can vary by species, by individual, from year to year, and by individual feathers on the same bird. Molts can be either complete, in which the bird replaces every one of its feathers over the same molt period; or partial, in which the bird replaces only some of its feathers (for example, flight feathers or body feathers). It takes a lot of energy to build new feathers. As a result, birds typically time their molts to avoid other periods of high energy demands, such as nesting or migration. [Ref 4-15]

Under the Humphrey–Parkes nomenclature for birds' plumages, the main adult plumage, especially when it is produced by a complete molt of flight and body feathers, is called basic plumage. In most birds, the non-breeding plumage (which is worn longer than the breeding plumage) is known as the basic plumage. In birds that molt only once a year, the regular and only plumage is known as basic plumage. In some birds, a partial molt occurs before the bird breeds. This plumage is known as the alternate plumage and is generally what was previously known as a bird's breeding plumage.

Birds such as warblers, tanagers, and buntings molt all their feathers after nesting and assume their basic plumage. Then, before the next breeding season, they have a partial molt of their body feathers that gives the males their bright alternate (breeding) plumage. Although the females don't typically molt into bright plumage, they still go through this same partial molt. [Ref 4-16]

In addition to providing a new set of healthy feathers, molts often provide a new look to the bird's plumage—new colors or patterns that can indicate the bird's age, sex, or the season of the year.

The number of times a year that birds molt varies by species. Examples of birds who undergo one complete molt per year are chickadees, flycatchers, hawks, hummingbirds, jays, owls, swallows, thrushes, vireos, and woodpeckers.

Only a few species undergo two full molts per year. Most of these birds live in areas where the environment causes significant feather wear and tear. Marsh Wrens and Bobolinks, two species that move through abrasive vegetation, are examples. [Ref 4-17]

Chapter 5 – Communicate

"Be still when you have nothing to say, when genuine passion moves you, say what you've got to say, and say it hot."

D. H. Lawrence

"Say a little and say it well."

Irish Proverb

"The more we elaborate our means of communication, the less we communicate.

J. B. Priestley

"Emotional awareness is necessary so you can properly convey your thoughts and feelings to the other person."

Jason Goldberg

"Communication involves self-revelation on the part of one individual and listening on the part of another."

Dr. Gary Chapman

Communication is the key to survival for many birds. By understanding each other, they can more easily find food, avoid danger, and stay in touch. They use communication for very practical and essential things, such as food, mating, territory, safety, and acknowledgement of their existence.

Birds communicate through their calls and songs, and through their body language and behavior. They use subtle clues in their body language to signal their intentions. For example, bobbing their heads up and down before taking flight.

Small birds must be very vigilant. As well as looking out for predators themselves, they need to react to sudden noises, or to alarm calls from other birds warning of predators in the area. (Ref 5-1)

Sound is a great form of bird communication because it can carry beyond where birds can see. When a bird sings, it can always be heard, even after it has moved out of sight. Sound travels in all directions. It can penetrate through or around objects.

Although birds can hear in a similar range to us, the noise they hear may be slightly different, Birds have excellent hearing. They can detect shorter and lower sounds than we can, which helps them to hear soft contact calls and recognize each other's songs. For example, they can pick out shorter notes in other birds' songs, so where these might appear to be one note to us, the bird could be hearing several shorter notes.

"Birds' ears, just like their eyes, take in information very quickly. If you record a simple birdcall and slow it down, you will discover all kinds of details that your ears didn't hear. Other birds probably can hear these extra sounds – otherwise there would be no reason for the birds to make them." (Ref 5-2)

The song of a Veery sounds very different if you listen at a human's normal speed and if you slow it down to quarter speed. The song is full of variations and complexities that birds hear.

Songbirds perform their songs using a specialized two-sided voice organ called a syrinx. Birds can have very complex vocalizations, often with more than one tone produced simultaneously, thanks to the specialized syrinx (their equivalent of a voice box) that allows them to create independent sounds in different parts of their trachea. (Ref 5-3)

The Wood Thrush *(Hylocichla mustelina)* song ends with one of the most complex sounds a bird can create. Layered above a series of lower-pitch mini-trills is a series of higher-pitch sweeping tones. To perform this impressive trill the bird must pair impeccably timed breath control with independent muscle movements on each side of the syrinx. [Ref 5-4]

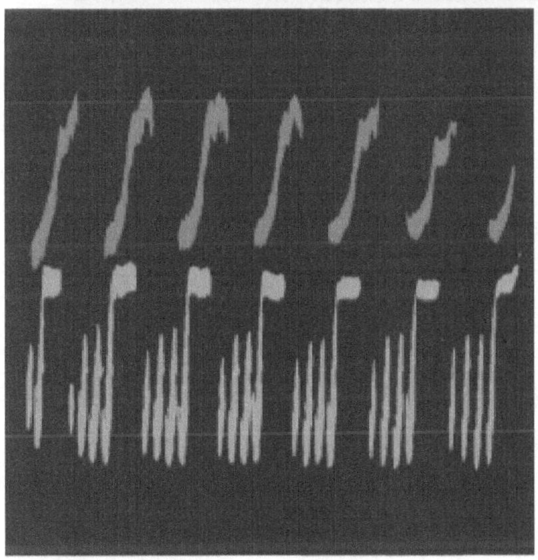

Figure 5-1 -Wood Thrush by Corey Hayes; song recording by Peter Paul Kellogg/Macaulay Library ML#11308, top and bottom indicate opposite sides of the syrinx.

Birds use a variety of call notes to convey different messages, such as alerting other birds to danger. Call notes are also used to locate their mate or offspring, or to communicate with other birds in their flock while flying. In smaller birds, call notes are often a chip, chirp, or peep, while in larger birds they may be a screech, caw, or click.

A large amount of bird communication involves nearby predators. Songbirds, especially, have long distance alarm calls that provide advanced warning of potentially dangerous predators in the area. Many birds have a high-pitched alarm call that they only use when an aerial predator is nearby. High-pitched sounds are difficult to locate, so the birds can give them without revealing their location.

Birds of one species recognize the alarm calls given by other species. When Black-capped Chickadees see a goshawk, owl, or some other winged predator, they issue an alarm call. This call varies depending on the level of the threat. If a raptor is flying far overhead, they issue a high-pitched "seet" call. If a perched raptor is seen nearby, they call "chick-a-dee-dee" with extra "dees" added if the threat appears especially dangerous. Other birds have learned to recognize and understand these warnings. This inter-species call recognition is not innate, but has to be learned. [Ref 5-5]

Flight calls are vocalizations made by birds while flying, often serving to keep flocks together.

Bird songs are differentiated from bird calls by complexity, length, and context. Songs are longer and more complex, and are associated with territory, courtship, and mating. Bird song is best developed in the order Passeriformes or birds that perch. It is usually delivered from prominent perches so the song will travel greater distances. Birds can sing at any time of day, but during the dawn chorus their songs are often louder and more frequent. The dawn chorus is mostly made up of male birds who are attempting to attract mates and warn other males away from their territories. In the early mornings, it is too dark to search for food and to be spotted by many predators—although night-hunting owls are an exception. (The author witnessed an American Robin singing loudly from a low fence just before dawn, who was picked up and carried off by a Great Horned Owl).

There are dangers to singing. It takes great energy to produce loud, clear notes, and the sounds can attract predators and make the singer more vulnerable. But the benefits birds get from singing – a prime territory, a healthy mate, and a place to raise their young – seem to generally be worth the risk.

Songbirds learn, practice, and perfect their songs, whereas the calls of other birds are hard-wired into them from birth and they don't perfect them.

Learning is required to produce complex songs. Songbirds learn their songs from listening to their parents. Songbirds and humans have a lot in common in this respect. Baby birds babble as human babies do. Like birds, humans need to hear themselves (and others) in order to produce normal adult sounds. And just as it is much harder for humans to learn languages after childhood, most songbirds experience a critical period as nestlings when they are best able to learn song.

There seem to be two critical times when songbirds learn their songs – during their first year of life, and during their first year of breeding. As nestlings, most songbirds listen to neighborhood songs and commit them to memory. It is only later, after they have fledged and moved to a new territory, that young birds begin to practice. These early practice songs are unclear and unstructured, similar to the babbling of a young child. After many months of practice, songbirds refine their songs and establish a repertoire, which often remains fixed for the remainder of their lives. [Ref 5-6]

Songs may last two to ten seconds or more and are often repeated in long sequences. A song is generally more musical than other calls, and often incorporates a range of pitches and rhythms into one connected sequence. Different bird species show great variety in the complexity and arrangement of their songs.

Birdsong structure and versatility vary enormously, from structurally simple songs with only one repeated element (e.g. Grasshopper Warblers) to highly complex songs (e.g. Nightingales) in which each male sings around 200 different song types, each of which is composed of many different elements. [Ref 5-7]

For the purpose of comparative studies, it is useful to categorize birds into continuous and discontinuous singers. Continuous singers such as Reed Warblers produce long, almost continuous streams of elements (the basic units of vocal production). The elements in the song repertoire of a continuous singer are usually recombined in various ways, so that each new sequence is slightly different from the previous ones.

Most male songbirds, however, are discontinuous singers. They alternate songs (which are a specific combination of song elements) with silent intervals. Among different species of discontinuous singers, there are two discrete singing styles. In some species, males repeat the same song type several times before switching to a song of a different type. This way of singing is most characteristic for species in which males have a small to medium repertoire of different song types (i.e., a repertoire of two to ten acoustically distinct songs). Birds following this repetitive mode are generally said to be singing with 'eventual variety.' Examples are Song Sparrows, Yellowhammers, Chaffinches, and Great Tits. [Ref 5-8]

In other species, males hardly ever repeat the same song type in immediate succession but instead, after each song, switch to a different song type within their repertoire. This singing style is referred to as showing 'immediate variety' and is characteristic of species that have larger song repertoires, such as Mockingbirds, European Blackbirds, or Nightingales. [Ref 5-9]

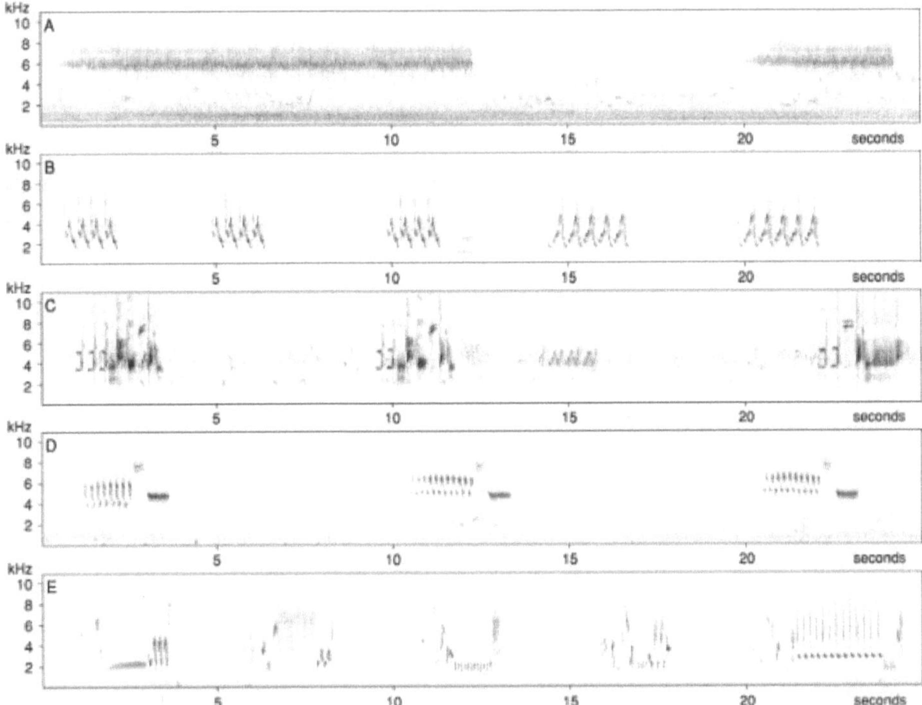

FIGURE 5-2 - SOUND spectrograms of singing sequences by males of five different species of songbirds. (A) Grasshopper warbler, *Locustella naevia*, (B) Carolina wren, *Thryothorus ludovicianus*, (C) song sparrow, *Melospiza melodia*, (D) yellowhammer, *Emberiza citrinella*, (E) nightingale, *Luscinia megarhynchos*; (B)–(D) show singers with eventual variety and (E) shows a species with immediate variety. (Ref 5-10)

Male birds learn songs from their parents and neighbors. But over time, some individuals might improvise and introduce variations, which are then picked up by the rest of the population, creating a regional dialect. Some songbird species develop distinct area-specific dialects. These local dialects are passed on to the next generation of birds. After many generations, the birds from one area can sound quite different from those in another area.

Birds hear their own songs and can make adjustments. Scientists say there is a noticeable difference in pitch between town and country bird song. They think bird song in the city is at a higher pitch to help reduce echoes bouncing off nearby buildings. (Ref 5-11)

Songbirds—with their two-sided voice boxes and capacity to learn complicated songs—have influenced many composers and instrumentalists. Bird melodies have been recreated by flutes, oboes, pianos, and xylophones in musical works from Haydn's *The Seasons* to Beethoven's sixth symphony.

Birds particularly fascinated Mozart, who kept a starling as a pet. According to one of his journals, he even taught the bird to sing the opening theme of one of his piano concertos (though it apparently always sang sharp.) This claim is believable as starlings are fantastic mimics, often boasting repertoires of 15–20 distinct imitations. Some reproductions are of different birds; while others are of manmade sounds such as cars, whistles, and even human speech. [Ref 5-12]

It is possible that birds enjoy their own songs. Given the complexity of birdsong and how birds go about it, some scientists have concluded that it is a mistake to think that songbirds sing only to attract a mate or defend a territory. They have theorized that birds may sometimes sing for the pleasure of it. When birds sing without territorial or courtship concerns, they may get enjoyment and comfort from singing.

Ofer Tchernichovski, a psychology professor at Hunter College in New York City, was waiting for a train to Manhattan when he heard a faint chirping. Looking around, he spotted a robin, fluttering on the platform. "His feathers were dull and he was all puffed up," Tchernichovski recalled. [Ref 5-13] "I don't think he could fly. It wasn't immediately apparent that he was singing—but he was." The song was quiet, but elaborate. Given the bird's condition, Tchernichovski thought that the bird might have been dying. But that didn't seem to stop him from singing. "It was kind of touching. He was definitely focused on singing, even though the song was not directed at anyone." Tchernichovski recalled gazing upon the dying robin at the train station with a mix of sadness and sanguine curiosity. At that moment, it certainly wasn't looking for a mate—and yet it was still singing. "This almost makes me feel better," Tchernichovski says. "It's as if the bird is somehow comforting itself. It seems to be more encouraged, even in sickness, by singing."

Swainson's Thrushes sing their haunting, upward-spiraling song continually, including while sitting on their nests. They may derive comfort from their songs while sitting for long hours on their nests.

The author spent many enjoyable minutes listening to Swainson's Thrushes singing at Mercer Slough near Seattle. Mercer Slough is the largest wetland expanse remaining on the east side of Seattle that remains connected to Lake Washington.

Swainson's Thrush

In the forested areas in Mercer Slough, I heard a bird singing over and over, but could not see it. Its song was a rising series of ephemeral, echoing flute-like notes rising higher and higher and ending in a haunting high note before gradually fading away. I often stood in the path amongst the trees and listened to the song for a long time, wondering how something could make such a different, beautiful, ephemeral sound:

trill — higher trill — higher trill — higher trill (with the highest trill carrying a double note or echo)

In June I had heard these birds constantly singing in the trees in Mercer Slough, but had not been able to locate one. During the first week of July, I finally saw one sitting on a branch above me, so that I had a good look at its underside. It was a light gray-brown bird with an oyster white belly and very light spots on its upper breast. It had very long legs. It was a Swainson's Thrush, which looks similar to the more cinnamon-brown colored Hermit Thrush, and also to the Veery, whose song is downward, instead of rising.

The Swainson's Thrush is a very shy, furtive ground living bird. It is heard more often than seen. Certain places in Mercer Slough met this bird's preferred habitat of damp coniferous forest edges or willow thickets found along creeks and sloughs (called riparian thickets).

The Swainson's Thrush sings on its nest, and I believe the birds that I heard singing over and over for a long time were sitting on nests. I was never able to see one of their nests, although the birds were singing close by the path.

FIGURE 5-3 – SWAINSON'S Thrush. Photo by the author.

Swainson's Thrushes sing their upward-spiraling, flutelike songs frequently in the summer. Their whirling song has a ventriloqual quality that makes it difficult to track. They also sometimes sing quiet songs that can create the illusion that their song is coming from a more distant location. They call frequently during fall and spring migrations to and from their wintering grounds in Central and northern South America, when their soft, bell-like overhead "peeps" may be mistaken for the calls of frogs.

Unquestionably, birds give us enormous pleasure listening to their songs and calls. The caroling of a robin cheers us up and the wail of a loon calling for its mate or young makes us pause and listen in awe.

Chapter 6 – Cooperate With Others

"In the long history of humankind (and animal kind, too) those who learned to collaborate and improvise most effectively have prevailed."

Charles Darwin

"Cooperation is willing collaboration by free individuals in a collective effort that creates more value than it expends."

James Raymond Lucas

"He that does good to another does good also to himself."

Lucius Annaeus Seneca

"In union there is strength."

Aesop

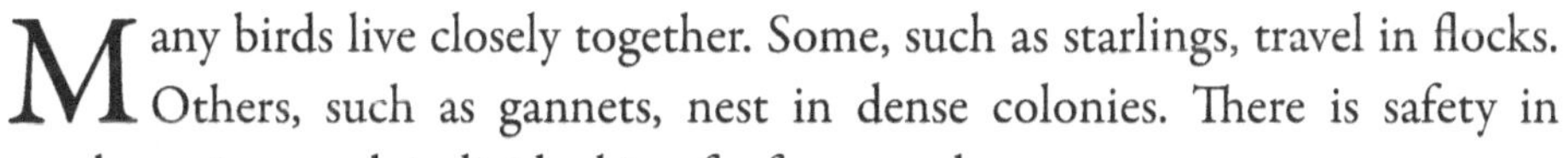

Many birds live closely together. Some, such as starlings, travel in flocks. Others, such as gannets, nest in dense colonies. There is safety in numbers, since each individual is safer from predators.

Some birds roost tightly together on cold nights to keep warm. Tiny Bushtits are social birds that live year-round in flocks of 10 to 40 birds, and roost huddled close together in a tight mass on cold nights.

Small birds cooperate to protect each other from predators. When a predator enters the area of a smaller bird, the smaller bird will alert others by screeching loudly. This is risky for the bird as the screeching draws the predator's attention. However, when other birds hear the call, they "mob" together around the predator, chasing it away. The more birds that join the mob, the more likely the predator will flee, and the quicker the smaller birds can return to their business.

Elegant Terns like to stay close to each other in large groups. They nest on the beaches of small islands at only four known sites: Bolsa Chica Ecological Reserve near Huntington Beach, California; Isla Rosa in the Gulf of California; San Diego Bay; and Los Angeles Harbor. Elegant Terns are considered vulnerable because their nesting is restricted to only a very few sandy or rocky islands. In late summer or early fall, after breeding, Elegant Terns move north along the coast, regularly to San Francisco, and rarely to British Columbia. Most move south again in October. Their wintering range extends as far south as Peru and northern Chile.

Elegant Terns forage by flying over the water, hovering and plunge-diving to catch prey below the surface. Feeding flocks of Elegant Terns are very noisy. Their calls are scratchy and grating and are given incessantly by flocks.

The author heard and saw flocks of these terns when they visited San Francisco Bay in September and October:

<u>*Elegant Terns*</u>

On September 15, 2012 I went along the Golden Gate Promenade about 8:00 am. For the past several weeks I had heard terns calling noisily as they flew along the waterfront. As I approached the Gulf of the Farallon's National Marine Sanctuary Visitor Center at the west end of Crissy Field, I saw hundreds of terns sitting on the pier behind the building.

FIG 6-1 – PIER BEHIND the Gulf of the Farallon's National Marine Sanctuary Visitor Center. Photo by the author.

A man was just coming out of the white building—which houses a National Oceanic and Atmospheric Administration (NOAA) office—next to the Gulf of the Farallon's Visitor Center. He headed towards the elevated walkway pier leading to a little shack. I heard him tell another man that the shack was where some kind of meeting was to take place. I asked the man if he knew what kind of terns were on the pier and said that I had noticed these small terns congregated on this pier about once a year. He answered that they were Elegant Terns and said: "If you want to get really nerdy and look through binoculars, you can see some smaller ones among them which are Least Terns". I commented the terns were very small – half the size of the Herring Gulls. He answered "Yes, aren't they gorgeous!" I felt very happy that someone shared my love of birds, as that is often the word I use to describe a bird – GORGEOUS!

On September 16, and again on September 22, 2012, there were 200 to 300 Elegant Terns along the pier. I saw one or two with the black feathers on their heads sticking up. I walked out on an adjacent parallel pier past the water line to look at them. I was alone and the surf pounded in below the pier. It felt very wild and a little scary, as I can't swim.

On September 29, 2012, there were no Elegant Terns on the pier. However, on October 14, 2012, once again many Elegant Terns were lined up, spaced closely together, on the pier. On some of them I saw the black feathers at the back of their heads sticking out. Several flew around and then landed. When they flew, their white tail feathers fanned out and appeared transparent.

A year later, on October 6, 2013, just before noon, I once again saw 100 to 200 Elegant Terns on the pier. I noticed that these terns liked to sit very close together. Although one end of the pier was vacant, the birds were bunched up at the far end. A tern would fly over and hover, and then gently settle down in a small space between two other birds. Usually, these birds were very noisy, continuously calling, taking off, and then landing again. However, on this day, they were almost completely silent and seemed to be resting at midday.

FIG 6-2 - ELEGANT TERNS resting on mud bar at Crissy Field Marsh. Photo by the author.

Human activities on beaches that are supposed to be protected can be extremely disruptive for the birds. Runaway dogs not on a leash chase them. Recreational drones that look like predators to the birds are a new threat.

The disastrous effect that a flying drone had on a colony of Elegant Terns nesting at one of their four known nesting beaches was recorded by Peter Knapp, a seasoned wildlife monitor with the California Department of Fish and Wildlife:

"On the morning of May 13, 2021 Knapp stepped onto an ominously quiet California beach. The night before, he'd noted a horde of boisterous Elegant Terns just starting to incubate their eggs in the Bolsa Chica Ecological Reserve, 30 miles south of Los Angeles. But the roughly 3,000 birds were missing.

'I didn't see the terns anywhere on the reserve,' said Knapp. 'So I started looking around.' [Ref 6-1]

By the time he reached North Tern Island, the birds' nesting site, he'd found the answer. On the ground was an illegal drone, which had obviously crashed. The birds did not return, abandoning some 1,500 sand nests, each holding one or two eggs.

'It was devastating. There was no other word.' said Melissa Loebl, the reserve manager at Bolsa Chica. [Ref 6-2]

Elegant Terns are especially sensitive to disruption during nesting season thanks to a couple of specific behaviors. First is flock density. 'Their one big anti-predator defense is to nest in these huge numbers,' says Kate Goodenough, a seabird ecologist at the University of Oklahoma. Every year, thousands of sleek, black-and-white Elegant Terns lay eggs along the beaches of small islands. Like New York City apartment tenants, they make the most of the available real estate, squeezing up to 5 nests in three square feet of sand.

The second behavior is known as group adherence. Unlike many bird species, an Elegant Tern's loyalty lies with the flock rather than the breeding ground itself. 'If some individuals take off for whatever reason, Goodenough says, 'the majority of the group also takes off and leaves.'" [Ref 6-3]

Scientists and wildlife managers did not know whether these Elegant Terns would try to renest this year at one of the other three known nesting sites for their species. They also did not know if they would come back to Bolsa Chica Ecological Reserve the next year.

FIGURE 6-3 - A PORTION of the thousands of Elegant Tern eggs abandoned in the Bolsa Chica Ecological Reserve. Photo: California Department of Fish and Wildlife.

After the drone crash scared them off their nests at the Bolsa Chica Reserve, the Elegant Terns established a new nesting colony atop two barges moored in Long Beach Harbor. This second nesting attempt ended up requiring intervention on the part of numerous wildlife organizations in order to save as many of the chicks as possible. (Ref 6-4)

It is suspected that fireworks over the July 4th long weekend scared the adult terns who then flew off the barges and into the water. The newly-hatched chicks tried to follow the adults. They fell off the high barges into the ocean. Once in the water, they were not able to make the high jump back up to the barge and were drowning in large numbers. People reported seeing cold and disoriented young Elegant Terns on the shoreline of Long Beach. International Bird Rescue, along with the California Department of Fish and Wildlife, the Oiled Wildlife Care Network, and other partners sprang into action to save as many of the chicks as they could.

Rescuers used varied and innovative methods. They tied low platforms, called haul-outs, to the barges. They chicks were able to climb onto these low platforms where they could wait to be fed by the adult terns.

FIG 6-4 - SPECIAL PLATFORMS, called haul-outs, were installed and tied off to barges in Long Beach Harbor. This gave young Elegant Terns an opportunity to climb onto one of 10+ platforms to get warm and wait for adults to feed them. Photo courtesy of Russ Curtis – International Bird Rescue.

Rescuers continually patrolled around the barges and picked up distressed chicks. Once picked up from the ocean, chicks were taken to International Bird Rescue's Los Angeles Oiled Bird Care and Education Center in San Pedro, where they were checked for fractures, fed, and warmed up before being returned to the breeding colony. They were given medicine to prevent pneumonia from inhaled seawater.

Adult Elegant Terns stay with their young in the colony for up to six months, teaching them to forage. International Bird Rescue tried to return as many of the young birds to the colony as soon as possible so that the adult birds could resume this critical role. The rescuers hoped to utilize the terns' natural "creche" nesting behavior—adults helping to raise young birds collectively—as they began to return the oldest, most fit chicks to the colony. [Ref 6-5]

In the month following this seabird crisis in Long Beach Harbor, over 2,500 chicks were saved, with more than 650 birds brought to the wildlife center for care, and others banded in the field or rescued by the innovative rescue platforms.

As of August 18 2021, 105 of the chicks at International Bird Rescue were too ill or injured to be returned to the colony and were to be raised by rescue staff before being released to the wild. [Ref 6-6] It is a great undertaking to successfully raise these chicks.

FIG 6-5 - THE TINIEST rescued Elegant Tern, "Little Mike" arrived weighing 60 grams, he is 92 grams in the picture. Photo courtesy of Kylie Clatterbuck – International Bird Rescue [Ref 6-7]

Before the chicks were released, they were given leg bands and were marked with a special paint which would disappear after a month. Citizen scientists were encouraged to report any of these marked birds in order to track how successful the chicks became subsequent to their rescue and release. One of the rescued and released marked birds was spotted in a large flock of terns at Malibu Lagoon State Park, which is 40 miles north of the original colony.

FIG 6-6 - AFTER INSTALLING special haul-outs near nesting barges, some rescued seabirds were well enough to be returned to the colony in Long Beach Harbor. The special pink marking aids monitoring. Photo courtesy of Kylie Clatterbuck – International Bird Rescue.

FIG 6-7 - ONE OF THE former Elegant Tern patients was spotted in a large flock at Malibu Lagoon State Park – some 40 miles north of the original colony. Photo courtesy of Trish Oster.

As well as cooperation among the same species of birds, association among different species of birds is common. Flocks of mixed species forage together for food in the winter. They defend territories together in alliances that can last for years.

In most cases, these partnerships between different species of birds are not between specific individuals of the other species – any bird from the other species will do. However, individual birds do recognize specific individuals of other species.

Researchers showed how birds from two different species recognized individuals and cooperated for their mutual benefit. [Ref 6-8] Two different species of Australian fairywrens not only recognized individual birds from the other species, but also formed long-term partnerships that helped them forage and defend their shared space as a group. Variegated Fairywrens and Splendid Fairywrens are two small non-migratory Australian songbirds that occupy territory in the same eucalyptus scrublands. Because Splendid and Variegated Fairywrens are so similar in their habitat preferences and behavior, they had been expected to act as competitors, but instead, the researchers found stable, positive relationships between individuals of the two species.

When their territories overlapped, the two species interacted with each other. They foraged together, traveled together, and seemed to be aware of what the other species was doing. They also helped each other defend their territory from unfamiliar birds of both species.

Both Splendid and Variegated Fairywrens demonstrated the ability to recognize their co-residents' songs despite the species difference. Socially dominant males of both species responded more aggressively to songs of neighbors and unknown birds than they did to friendly birds sharing their territory. When they heard songs from friendly birds, they didn't respond, suggesting they didn't see them as a threat.

By forming and keeping these associations with another species, Fairywrens could better defend their nests from predators and their territories from rivals. There was also evidence that interacting with the other species had additional benefits besides territorial defense. While the Splendid Fairywrens didn't change their behavior when associating with the other species, the Variegated Fairywrens spent more time foraging, were less vigilant, and had more success raising their young.

The researchers believed the Fairywrens associate with the other species as a form of cooperation. By interacting with other species that share the same territory instead of working against them, these already social species create a larger group to help defend their territory and ward off intruders.

One of the authors of the study commented: [Ref 6-9] "Although our discovery that individuals of different species recognize each other was unexpected, it is likely that something similar occurs whenever species of non-migratory birds live on overlapping territories. Recognition facilitates sociality within species, and it follows that it could also facilitate associations between species."

The author witnessed the interactions of a Long-billed Curlew and a Western Willet who occupied the same territory at Crissy Field Marsh in San Francisco over numerous winters:

<u>*Friendship Between a Long-billed Curlew and a Western Willet*</u>

These two birds often fed and rested close to one another in the marsh. They seemed to be friends. One day in August the Willet's feathers looked ruffled and its demeanor showed that it felt uncomfortable. The author believed that it was molting. The Long-billed Curlew was standing a little distance away and looking at the Willet. Then they both started to preen at the same time.

FIGURE 6-8 – THE LONG-billed Curlew and the Western Willet preening together 1. Photo by the author.

FIGURE 6-9 – THE LONG-billed Curlew and the Western Willet preening together 2. Photo by the author.

Long-billed Curlews will occasionally lay eggs in the nests of other Long-billed Curlews, and the Long-billed Curlew and Willet have been known to lay eggs in each other's nests. [Ref 6-10]

In *Life Histories of North American Birds*, Arthur Cleveland Bent [Ref 6-11] stated that A. O. Treganza, from Utah, had found sometimes two female Long-billed Curlews sharing the same nest, resulting in sets of from five to eight eggs. In one instance he found four eggs of the Western Willet and one of the Curlew in a nest, with both the Willet and the Curlew on guard.

Arthur Cleveland Bent (1866-1954)

Arthur Cleveland Bent was a successful businessman and a dedicated amateur ornithologist. In 1901 he began submitting papers to "The Auk", the journal of the American Ornithologists' Society (formerly the American Ornithologists' Union). In 1910, he approached the Secretary of the Smithsonian Institution with a proposal to undertake, at his own expense, the completion of a series started by Charles E. Bendire, who had issued the first volume of "Life Histories of North American Birds". (Ref 6-12). Bent was 44 years old at the time of his proposal, and he dedicated the remaining 44 years of his life to completing this impressive endeavor.

As a businessperson with a strong work ethic and highly developed organizational skills, Bent was thorough and meticulous in his research. He organized the life history data for each species in a uniform sequence, including Spring Migration, Courtship, Nesting Habits, Eggs, Young, Sequence of Plumages to Maturity, Seasonal Molts, Feeding Habits, Flight, Swimming and Diving Habits, Vocal Powers, Behavior, Enemies, Fall Migration, and Winter Habits.

What Bent originally believed would take six volumes to complete when he began work on his "Life Histories of North American Birds" in 1910, proliferated into 20 volumes by the time of his death in 1954, with a few remaining volumes in the series later completed under the supervision of ornithologist Oliver L. Austin, Jr. This comprehensive work contains hundreds of avian species biographies.

Bent supplemented his own observations with the published literature and unpublished notes of a network of volunteer contributors and collaborating authors. In order to recruit contributors to his "Life Histories of North American Birds", Bent mailed out countless circulars and advertised repeated requests in ornithological publications. The favorable initial response encouraged him to continue with the project. Over 150 people contributed eggs, notes, and/or photographs for the first volume published in 1919. Bent corresponded with hundreds of ornithologists while accumulating information for his life histories. (Ref 6-13) He always acknowledged the names of these collaborators, and by the end of the project, contributions had been received from over 800 author partners.

The Bent series remains a starting point for serious research on the life history of North American birds. Also, it is far from dry reading. It contains an abundance of readable descriptions of the lives of birds, written by a large number of enthusiastic nature lovers and observers of birds in the field. It is interesting to note that A. C. Bent did not have formal training in ornithology and never received a salary for his monumental work, which none the less won great praise from the ornithological community and remains a standard reference work to this day.

In Bent's *Life Histories*, W. H. Hudson described a Solitary Sandpiper and a blue [American] Bittern sharing their lives as follows: [Ref 6-14]

"I was once pleased and much amused to discover in a small, sequestered pool in a wood, well sheltered from sight by trees and aquatic plants, a Solitary Sandpiper living in company with a blue [American] Bittern. The bittern patiently watched for small fishes and when not fishing, dozed on a low branch overhanging the water, while its companion ran briskly along the margin snatching up minute insects from the water. When disturbed they rose together, the bittern with its harsh, grating scream, the sandpiper daintily piping its fine, bright notes – a wonderful contrast! Every time I visited the pool afterwards, I found these two hermits, one so sedate in manner the other so lively, living peacefully together."

Groups of birds often flock together. Celeste Silling explains why they may do this [Ref 6-15]: "For centuries, humans have wondered how and why birds move in coordinated groups across huge distances. We know now that there are many advantages to flocking and various species get various benefits depending on how they flock. Flocking helps birds notice and defend against predators, as they can all look in different directions to see threats. In addition, if a predator should come upon a flock, it can be distracted and confused by the swirling bodies and have a more difficult time picking out a single prey bird to target.

Some species flock in formations that give them special benefits. Geese fly in a V formation that enables them to spend less energy flying across long distances. When the bird at the front of the V flaps its wings, the bird behind it benefits from the updraft that it creates, similar to the wake following behind a boat. Each bird in turn creates its own wake, making it easier for the bird behind to fly. If a goose drops out of the V, it will feel the full impact of the air, encouraging it to get back in the formation. In this way, geese know that it is better to flock together, especially for those that are weaker or smaller. Stronger and larger geese will tend to take the lead of the V formation, but they don't always remain in front for the whole journey. When the leader grows tired, it will rotate back to an arm of the V and a new leader will take its place."

Starlings can flock in huge, tightly connected masses called murmurations. These murmurations appear both chaotic and synchronized, moving erratically but as one. Researchers have discovered that starlings in these murmurations coordinate with the seven closest birds around them. This number can change depending on the size and shape of the flock, but seven seems to be the most effective and common number. By looking at only the birds nearest to themselves, starlings can send waves of information through the flock. If a bird on the edge sees a predator and moves away from it, it will only take seconds before the birds on the other side of the group know to move in that direction too without ever having seen the predator for themselves. (Ref 6-16)

Flocking is so advantageous that birds of different species often opt to flock together. "With a mixture of species comes a mixture of special abilities. For example, when Red-eyed Vireos, who are nearsighted, flock with Yellow-margined Flycatchers, who are farsighted, the group as a whole can see predators at any distance. The combination of different senses, hunting abilities, and other specialized characteristics can give the group a huge advantage when migrating across great distances. When it comes to flocking, the sum is certainly greater than its parts, which is why so many birds can be seen doing it." (Ref 6-17)

Young birds migrating for the first time over open water may gain an advantage by joining a mixed flock of birds migrating in the same direction.

In a number of bird species, search for food occurs underwater. A typical dive cycle includes underwater time, during which individuals travel to the foraging area, search for food, and return to the surface, as well as surface time between these foraging episodes needed to recover from a prolonged period of time spent underwater.

Individuals in flocks of Surf Scoters and Barrow's Goldeneyes tend to dive and surface at the same time together. When one individual dives, the others quickly follow. This may allow the birds to follow one another to localized food patches of prey such as mussels. It also may help an individual to gain protection from having its prey stolen by gulls when it surfaces. (Ref 6-18)

Chapter 7 – Have Courage in the Face of Danger

"Bravery is not a quality of the body. It is of the soul."

Mahatma Gandhi

"The stronger your principles and values, the more you're willing to die for them."

Maxime Lagacé

"Necessity makes even the timid brave."

Sallust

"Courage is almost a contradiction in terms. It means a strong desire to live taking the form of a readiness to die."

G. K. Chesterton

"Cowards die many times before their deaths, the valiant never taste of death but once."

William Shakespeare

"You do not need to know precisely what is happening, or exactly where it is all going. What you need is to recognize the possibilities and challenges offered by the present moment, and to embrace them with courage, faith and hope."

Thomas Merton

"The only alternative to shuddering paralysis is to leap into action regardless of the consequences."

Alan Watts

In spite of fear of danger or pain, courage requires the mental fortitude to carry on with a commitment, plan, or decision, knowing it is the right or best course of action. Courage consists of acknowledging fear, and continuing through the fear.

Life for a bird is serious. The game of life in the wild is to survive and reproduce, to eat and not to get eaten. It is a surprisingly hard game, and most individual birds lose.

The life of a bird is fraught with dangers, which birds bravely attempt to overcome. Dr. Henry Smith Williams explained that the prosperity of any species depends upon the balance between its birth rate and its death rate: (Ref 7-1) "Even a seemingly prosperous species may meet local conditions with which it is quite unable to cope, and may disappear, for want of timely aid, from a region where it was once abundant, as our Orchard Orioles and Bobolinks, and Red-headed Woodpeckers and Bobwhites have disappeared.

A single red squirrel may reduce by half or wholly annul for the season, the increase of a whole colony of Robins, Catbirds, and Chipping Sparrows. A single black snake may bring similar disaster to other colonies of these species, or to Song Sparrows, Meadowlarks, Redwings, and Thrashers. A single Cowbird may bring about an infant mortality rate close to 100 percent in the households of four or five pairs of Maryland Yellowthroats, Prairie Warblers, Redstarts, Louisiana Water Thrushes or Warbling Vireos. Five years of such marauding, unopposed, and half the species of our bird colony might be exterminated; the other half reduced to a remnant. A bird that raises large broods or multiple broods in a season, and yet does not seem to increase in numbers year by year, must live very dangerously."

In *Survival by the Numbers*, the Cornell Lab of Ornithology wrote the following sobering analysis: (Ref 7-2)

<u>Life is Hard – Follow the story of 100 Red-winged Blackbird eggs</u>:

1. 100 Red-winged Blackbird eggs.
2. Due to predators, such as minks, racoons, and grackles, as well as other possible hazards, only 40 percent of those eggs hatch.
3. From here, another 60 percent will likely fall prey to predators, such as hawks, owls, and snakes.
4. So, of the 40 chicks that hatched, only 16 will live long enough to successfully fledge.
5. Life is hard for these 16 surviving fledglings. In the year it takes to become old enough to breed, only **<u>ONE</u>** will successfully reach breeding age and be able to start the cycle again.

Many bird species will act courageously in the face of danger to themselves or to their offspring. Adult birds invest a great deal of their life's energy in their offspring, and they will act bravely to defend them from harm, even if that means putting their own lives in danger.

When a predator comes close to a nesting Killdeer, the adult leaves the nest, attracting attention to itself by uttering distress calls. It drags a wing on the ground, giving the appearance of a broken wing, and slowly flutters along the ground, luring the intruder away from its nest or young.

Many species of small birds will swoop down or dash at a flying or perched larger bird who is a potential predator. Common mobbers include chickadees, titmice, kingbirds, blackbirds, grackles, jays, and crows. Hawks, owls, ravens, and herons are common targets of mobbing. A group of birds may harass a perched predator in order to encourage it to move to another area. Intense mobbing behavior is often directed towards perched owls, who often prey on sleeping birds. Smaller birds try to chase these predators from their territories so they can be safer at night. Blackbirds or kingbirds may make contact with larger potential predators as they drive them off. Mobbing behavior is not as dangerous to the smaller birds as it may appear, as the greater maneuverability of the mobber, and the lack of surprise by the predator, take away much of the predator's advantage.

A comment from a reader on one of The Cornell Lab's *All About Birds* sites follows: [Ref 7-3] "A hawk lives nearby and is relentlessly picking off baby Blue Jays living in a big spruce on my property. Amazingly, the adult Blue Jays and dozens of Red-winged Blackbirds work together to mob the hawk—the Red-winged Blackbirds will fly from all over to get in on the action.... the hawk has not been deterred. I think he's picked the whole brood off at this point. He is a juvenile hawk and I imagine he is sowing his oats. It is something to see the birds work together to defend the nest, though."

Alexander Wilson, the "father of North American ornithology", in 1832 described a Spotted Sandpiper's brave defense of her young as follows: [Ref 7-4]

"My venerable friend, Mr. William Bartram, informs me that he saw one of these birds defend her young for a considerable time from the repeated attacks of a ground squirrel. The scene of action was on the river shore. The parent had thrown herself, with her two young behind her, between them and the land, and at every attempt of the squirrel to seize them by a circuitous sweep raised both her wings in an almost perpendicular position, assuming the most formidable appearance she was capable of, and rushed forwards on the squirrel, who, intimidated by her boldness and manner, instantly retreated; but presently returning was met, as before, in front and on flank by the daring and affectionate bird, who with her wings and whole plumage bristling up seemed swelled to twice her usual size. The young crowded together behind her, apparently sensible of their perilous situation, moving backward and forward as she advanced or retreated. This interesting scene lasted for at least ten minutes; the strength of the poor parent began evidently to flag, and the attacks of the squirrel became more daring and frequent, when my good friend, like one of those celestial agents who in Homer's time so often decided the palm of victory, stepped forward from his retreat, drove the assailant back to his hole, and rescued the innocent from destruction."

Arthur Cleveland Bent describes the courage of the Long-billed Curlew in protecting its young from a predator as follows: [Ref 7-5] "Probably the mortality of many young Curlews is rather high, as they have many enemies.

All three of the broods we found contained only two young. The parents have to work hard to preserve even this average. We saw an interesting exhibition of parental strategy one day, which probably succeeded in saving some young Curlews from the jaws of a prowling coyote. The Curlew was decoying the coyote away by feigning lameness, flopping along the ground a few yards ahead of him, but always managing to barely escape him. We watched them for some time until they finally disappeared over a hill, fully half a mile from where we first saw them."

Sometimes, a bird's courage is carried a notch higher, and becomes bravery and heroism. Courage is that firmness of spirit which meets danger, acknowledging fear, but continuing through the fear. Bravery is daring, often defiant, courage. Heroism is contempt of danger from a noble and self-forgetful devotion.

A scientific paper [Ref 7-6] documented the heroism of an Eastern Meadowlark who aggressively defended its nest from a snake. Aggressive defense was defined as a bird's diving and pecking in close proximity to a predator, during which the bird could be injured or killed.

When the color-banded Eastern Meadowlark attacked a Western Fox snake, the snake caught the Meadowlark by the leg and held the bird for 43 seconds. Subsequently, the Meadowlark escaped, returned after eight seconds, and resumed attacking the snake. In total, the bird struck the snake 198 times with its bill during a 15-minute period, and, in this case, succeeded in driving the snake from its nest.

If this does not demonstrate heroism, the author does not know what would.

                    VAL SHUSHKEWICH

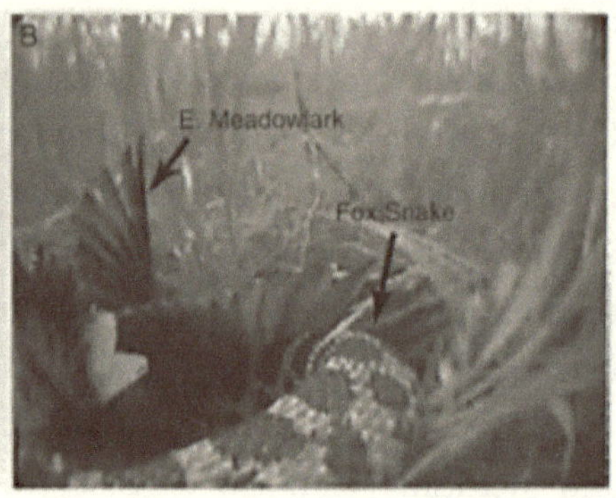

FIGURE 7-1 - ELLISON, Kevin and Ribic, Christine, "Nest Defense – Grassland Bird Responses to Snakes" (2012). USGS Northern Prairie Wildlife Research Center. 252.

Chapter 8 – Persevere

"The day you give up on your dreams is the day you give up on yourself."

Author Unknown

"It's not that I'm so smart, it's just that I stay with problems longer."

Albert Einstein

"When you are going through hell, keep on going. Never, never, never give up."

Winston Churchill

"When you feel like giving up, remember why you held on for so long in the first place."

Author Unknown

Perseverance means to persist in any enterprise undertaken, in spite of counter influences, opposition, and other setbacks.

Breeding birds will often try again after they have a setback. Their goal is to raise healthy offspring who will be able to carry on their species. Birds may carefully construct a nest only to have it destroyed in a storm. They then may build a new nest and lay eggs, only to have them taken by a predator. If the female and male are still alive, they may try again, and the eggs may hatch, only to have the nestlings taken by predators. If there is still time in the birds' breeding season, they may try yet another time, and hopefully will see their fledglings successfully try their wings and fly away. As long as they are able to, breeding birds persevere in trying to attain their goal of creating healthy offspring.

Migrating birds are motivated to begin their migrations by innate biological factors. However, once their journey has begun, they need persistence and perseverance to continue until they reach their goal. Migration is a huge feat of endurance requiring great strength and stamina. Once a bird has begun a long-distance migratory flight, giving up is not an option. It must keep on going until it reaches its destination. Fortunately, some birds make it through and can fulfill their dreams.

Storms are the greatest hazard facing migrating birds. Birds that cross broad stretches of water can confront headwinds associated with a storm, become exhausted, and fall into the waves. A catastrophe like this was once witnessed from the deck of a vessel in the Gulf of Mexico, thirty miles from the mouth of the Mississippi River. Great numbers of migrating birds, mostly warblers, were nearing land. They had accomplished 95 percent of their long flight. But they were caught by a "norther" – a sudden, cold gale from the north. The birds could not make headway against the storm. Hundreds were forced into the waters of the Gulf and drowned. A sudden drop in temperature accompanied by a snowfall can cause a similar effect.

Today birds face additional threats caused by human activity. Hungry and exhausted birds may arrive at a stopover site to find that it has been destroyed by farming or urbanization. Every year, millions of birds are illegally killed by hunters, or they collide with man-made structures such as lighthouses, tall buildings, television towers, power lines, and wind turbines.

Climate change is causing habitats to shift or disappear. Climate change may cause deserts to expand, creating additional obstacles to migrating birds suffering from dehydration, who are then forced to fly further over inhospitable landscapes.

Whimbrels are extreme long-distance migrants. There are two distinct North American breeding areas – one along the northern Alaska coast, Yukon and Mackenzie Delta, and another west and south of Hudson Bay. Like many other tundra breeders, those in the East fly offshore over the Atlantic during their autumn migration to South America, returning in spring mainly along an interior continental route, while it was assumed that those in the West migrated along the West Coast in the fall.

FIGURE 8-1- WHIMBREL Range Map (from *Birds of the World*).

In spring, a group of Whimbrels stage along the lower Delmarva Peninsula in Virginia and feed on fiddler crabs to gain the weight needed for the tremendous amount of energy used on a long-distance flight. It had previously been assumed that all of this group of Whimbrels were from the North American eastern Hudson Bay breeding population. However, in 2008 the Center for Conservation Biology at the College of William and Mary, and The Nature Conservancy in Virginia tracked a female Whimbrel named Winnie by satellite from Virginia all the way to the Mackenzie River area.

Winnie the Whimbrel surprised researchers by flying nonstop from her staging area in Virginia to the Mackenzie River area. This documented a previously unknown to science and entirely unexpected migration route between the mid-Atlantic coast and the northwestern Arctic. She completed the flight of more than 3,200 miles in 146 hours, sustaining an average flight speed of 22 miles per hour for six days.

FIGURE 8-2 - MIGRATION path of Winnie the Whimbrel. Credit: The Center for Conservation Biology.

After Winnie made her record-setting trip to the Mackenzie River, she continued to her breeding grounds in Alaska's Colville River system above the Arctic Circle. She remained on her breeding grounds from June 7 to July 12 when she began moving west along the northern Alaska coast. She staged in the west coast of Alaska until August 2, when she flew south over the north Pacific. Here, she flew into a cyclone and turned east to Willapa Bay in Washington State, where she stayed for two weeks to rest and refuel. From here, researchers expected her to fly south down the Pacific Coast, but instead she turned towards the east again, on what would be the last of her great migratory flights. After flying east for another thousand miles and up to seven days, her satellite receiver became stationary in Wisconsin around Lake Superior.

Bryan Watts, Director of William and Mary's Center for Conservation Biology believes she encountered stiff headwinds over the high plains, ended up in a poor foraging area and "just ran out of gas". He said: "How frequently this sort of thing happens, we have no idea. We have evidence of major die-offs over the Atlantic where some birds go out and the storm comes and lots of carcasses wash up. To be lost in a place where you don't have much to feed on, that's a risk that the birds take." [Ref 8-1]

Another example of the amazing migrations undertaken by Whimbrels was documented in 2012 by three Whimbrels tracked by scientists at the Center for Conservation Biology and the Canadian Wildlife Service. [Ref 8-2] The three birds were originally satellite marked on their breeding grounds along the Mackenzie River Delta in far western Canada. In mid-July, the birds flew across the continent to the east coast of Canada and staged for approximately two weeks to build fat reserves. They then flew southeast out over the Atlantic Ocean, reaching the center of the Atlantic Ocean before turning south and reaching landfall in South America between Guyana and Brazil. Their migration route passed through the center of the vast Atlantic Ocean and at one point it was one thousand miles closer to Africa than to North America. Although this portion of the Atlantic is used by true seabirds that roost on the water, it is so isolated from shore that species such as Whimbrels that cannot land on water were not believed to reach it.

One of the Whimbrels, named Mackenzie, averaged 30 miles an hour for the six days of the nonstop 4,300-mile flight.

The birds might have received some benefit from venturing this far out to sea in the form of favorable tailwinds. Also, this behavior may have arisen as a successful way to skirt past the hurricane-prone Caribbean.

Much has yet to be discovered about the mysteries of bird migration.

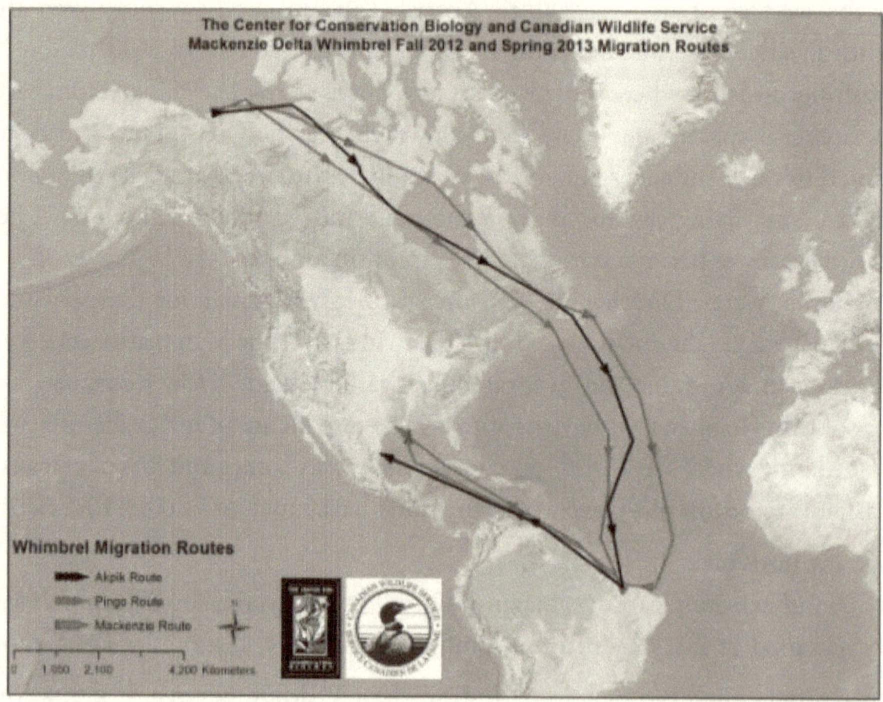

Figure 8-3 - Tracking map – Map of Mackenzie River Whimbrel movements July 2012 through June 2013. Birds have been tracked using solar-powered satellite transmitters. Map by The Center for Conservation Biology (CCB).

Chapter 9 – Have Confidence

"If you are to succeed in life, you must believe that you can succeed. That self-belief lifts you up."

Benjamin Kofi Quansah

"You have to have confidence in your ability, and then be tough enough to follow through."

Rosalynn Carter

"Life is not easy for any of us. But what of that? We must have perseverance and above all confidence in ourselves. We must believe that we are gifted for something and that this thing, at whatever cost, must be attained."

Marie Curie

"If I have lost confidence in myself, I have the universe against me."

Ralph Waldo Emerson

"Beyond a wholesome discipline, be gentle with yourself. You are a child of the universe no less than the trees and the stars; you have a right to be here."

Desiderata, Max Ehrmann © 1927

Confidence means believing in yourself, feeling comfortable with who you are, and recognizing that you have worth and a right to be here. With self-confidence, you believe you can do something. Your chances of accomplishing what you set out to do increase with your self-confidence and your determination to make it happen.

Adult birds seem to take the ability to fly for granted. They seem to fly effortlessly and unconsciously. But a bird needs to learn how to fly, and this often involves trial and error for young birds because the mechanics of flight rely not only on instinct but also on practice. Similar to how a human baby's first steps are interrupted with frequent stumbles and falls, baby birds don't learn to fly in a day. A young bird exercises its wings to make them stronger, and eventually it has the self-confidence it needs to take flight. It believes it can fly.

As a developing young bird approaches fledging, its parents may start withholding food, perching with food near the nest, or flying over with food to tempt the nestlings to leave the nest. Adults may also encourage nestlings through vocalizations and low circling over and around the nest. When the nestlings are hungry, thirsty, or confident enough, they fledge. First flights are often rather awkward and many fledging attempts are less than successful and the young bird is stuck on the ground. The parents typically continue to feed the grounded bird who eventually does fly again. Its first attempts at flying may be awkward and irregular, but as it keeps going, it learns to exercise control over its actions until it can fly without conscious thought over every movement.

Professional speaker and photographer Steve Kaye wrote the following about the confidence of a bird he saw perched on a branch: [Ref 9-1]

"When I saw this bird, I wondered what choice it had made to perch on that branch. So, I asked:

'Hey there, why did you hop up on that branch?'

'Because I knew I could. And that's also why I can fly – because I know I can.'

'What if you didn't know you could?'

'Then I'd be stuck on the ground. You see, every choice forward begins with confidence in yourself. So, if you want to rise above where you are, you must know that you can. You might conclude that knowing you can is the first choice you make on your way to achieving success.'

'Does every bird know this?'

'Of course! Every bird has optimism built into its instinct for survival.'

And with that, the bird flew away."

A scene from the Public Broadcasting System movie *Nature: Magic of the Snowy Owl* [Ref 9-2] showed a female Snowy Owl leading her three owlets, who could not yet fly, across the tundra to the coast where prey was more abundant. The three owlets trundled across the tundra following their mother. At one point they came to a deep, turbulent small river. The mother Snowy Owl could fly across, but the three fledglings stood on the bank and did not know what to do. One of the owlets boldly plunged into the river and swam across using its wings. The other two owlets stood on the bank and watched it. After much hesitation, a second owlet followed suit. The third owlet needed to gather its confidence. It entered the water, and then turned around and retreated to the bank. After waiting there some time, it finally found the confidence it needed and entered the river, determined to use its wings to swim across the river. It made it to the other side.

Chapter 10 – Have Patience

"Adopt the pace of nature: her secret is patience."

Ralph Waldo Emerson

"Patience is power. Patience is not an absence of action; rather it is 'timing'. It waits on the right time to act, for the right principles, and in the right way."

Fulton J. Sheen

"The keys to patience are acceptance and faith. Accept things as they are, and look realistically at the world around you. Have faith in yourself and in the direction you have chosen."

Ralph Marson

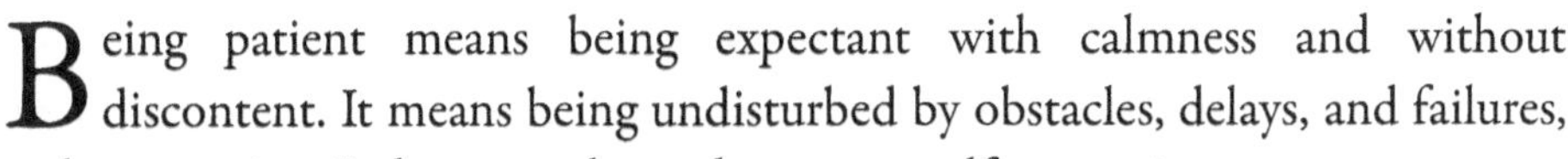

Being patient means being expectant with calmness and without discontent. It means being undisturbed by obstacles, delays, and failures, and persevering. It denotes calm endurance or self-possession.

Great Blue Herons are the largest heron in North America. Their average lifespan in the wild is 15 years, and the oldest recorded Great Blue Heron was 24 years old.

The Great Blue Heron, a master of patience, waits to secure its meal. It forages mostly by standing still or walking very slowly in shallow water, waiting for fish to swim near, then striking with a rapid thrust of the bill. It also forages on shore, from floating objects, and in grassland. It may hunt by day or night. (Ref 10-1)

In western Florida, the Great Blue Heron "can be seen hunting in areas with alligators looming in the distance. Their keen eyesight not only allows them to be successful hunters, it also keeps them aware of any potential dangers lurking nearby. It is no wonder that the Great Blue Heron is able to survive throughout such a broad geographic range including most of North America." (Ref 10-2)

In 1921, W. J. Erichsen described the Great Blue Heron in the winter on the coast of Georgia: (Ref 10-3) "The greater portion of its food is secured from the salt marshes and the banks and shallows of the numerous creeks that wind their way through them. It is often seen in company of the smaller herons, particularly the little blue species. At such times it is the first to take wing at the approach of danger, and usually is far away before the intruder has arrived within 100 yards of the spot where it stood. Upon stationing itself in a shallow creek to secure passing fish, if the latter are scarce the bird will remain motionless in one spot for a long period of time, apparently sluggish, and in an indifferent attitude; but when the fish are plentiful it becomes very active, spearing them right and left in rapid succession."

In his *Life Histories of North American Marsh Birds* (Ref 10-4), A. C. Bent said about the Great Blue Heron: "It is a stately bird, dignified in its bearing, graceful in its movements and an artistic feature in the landscape...In its native solitudes, far from the haunts of man, it may be seen standing motionless, in lonely dignity, on some far distant point that breaks the shore line of a wilderness lake, its artistic outline giving the only touch of life to the broad expanse of water and its background of somber forest. Or on some wide, flat coastal marsh its stately figure looms up in the distance, as with graceful, stealthy tread it wades along in search of its prey. Perhaps you have seen it from afar and think you can gain a closer intimacy, but its eyes and ears are keener than yours; and it is a wise and wary bird. But even as it takes its departure, you will stand and admire the slow and dignified strokes of its great, black-tipped wings, until this interesting feature of the landscape fades away into the distance. A bird so grand, so majestic, and so picturesque is surely a fitting subject for the artist's brush."

The Great Blue Heron can adapt to almost any wetland habitat in its range. It may be found in fresh and saltwater marshes, mangrove swamps, flooded meadows, lake edges, or shorelines. It may be seen in heavily developed areas as long as they hold bodies of fish-bearing water. With its variable diet, it is able to spend the winter farther north than most herons, even in areas where most waters freeze, but it must be careful not to get caught in an area that becomes completely frozen over. Sometimes an adult Great Blue Heron will be caught by a sudden winter storm and freeze-up, in which it cannot get to its regular food supply. In this case, it will often choose to wait out the freeze until it can get its food at its favorite feeding spot again. The wait may be too long.

The author often saw Great Blue Herons standing in the tall grass in Crissy Field, or wading in Crissy Field Marsh:

Great Blue Heron

In the spring of 2018, I noticed a Great Blue Heron fly into one of the Eucalyptus trees which form a line along the edge of the field by the St. Francis Yacht Club. When I looked at the spot where the Heron had landed, I saw a nest high up in the tree. This area becomes crowded with people, especially later in the day and on weekends when people set up nets on the grass and play volleyball. However, all this activity below them didn't seem to affect the herons in successfully raising their young.

FIGURE 10-1 - GREAT Blue Heron nest in Eucalyptus tree at the start of the Golden Gate Promenade in San Francisco. Photo by the author.

FIGURE 10-2 - GREAT Blue Heron at edge of Crissy Field Marsh. Photo by the author.

FIGURE 10-3 - GREAT Blue Herons in Crissy Field Marsh. Photo by the author.

Building a bird's nest requires great patience and craftsmanship. Birds gather grasses and twigs and assemble them into a nest cup, weaving bits and pieces together. Some bird nests, such as those of orioles and bushtits, are works of art.

In her book *A-Birding on a Bronco*, Florence Merriam described a Bushtit's nest which was on the ground: [Ref 10-5] "On taking it home and pulling it to pieces, I found that the wall was from half an inch to an inch thick, made of fine gray moss and oak blossoms. There was a thick wadding of feathers inside. I counted three hundred, and there were a great many more. The amount of hard labor this stood for amazed me."

FIGURE 10-4 – BUSHTIT nest hanging from a tree along path by footbridge over Still Creek in Burnaby, British Columbia. Photo by the author.

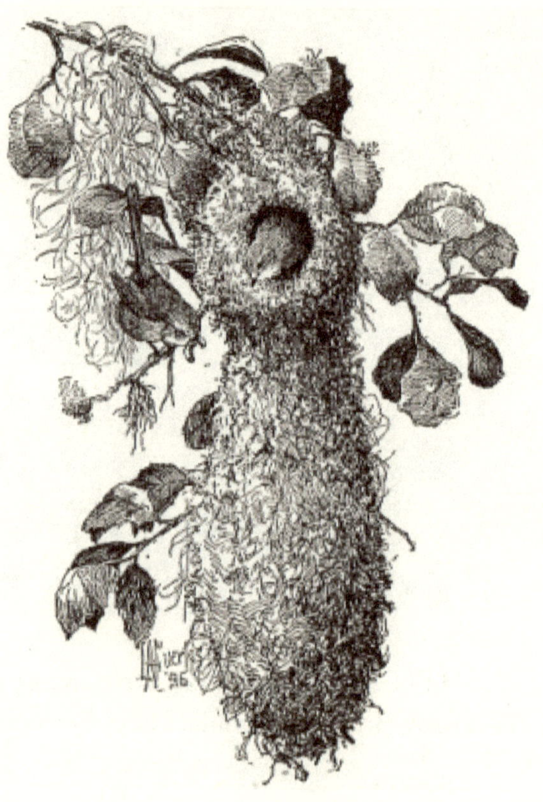

FIGURE 10-5 – NEST of the Bushtit. From *A-Birding on a Bronco* by Florence A. Merriam, 1896. (Drawing by Louis Agassiz Fuertes)

Baltimore Orioles build remarkable, sock-like hanging nests, woven together from slender fibers. The weaving process requires patience and finesse. The female weaves the nest. She anchors her nest high in a tree, winding long fibers around a branch to create the support strands for the rest of the structure. Then the female makes a series of rapid thrust and draw movements with her beak to begin forming the pouch. While no knots are deliberately tied, soon the random poking has made knots and tangles, and the female brings more fibers to extend, close, and finally line the nest. Building the nest takes about a week, but windy or rainy weather may extend this to as long as 15 days. Males occasionally bring nesting material.

"It's absolutely fascinating to sit and watch them weave," says Nancy Flood, a biologist who has studied orioles for 40 years. "You see the female poking one end of the string through, and then pulling her head back to weave it out, just like when you crochet or knit a bag. They can spend half an hour doing that, then go away to get another long piece of grass and do more." (Ref 10-6)

Nest materials vary. Females will choose whatever's immediately available around the breeding site. Kenn Kaufman once watched a Baltimore Oriole return to a patch of swamp milkweed for three days straight, each time stripping off long, strong fibers from the plants to weave into its nest.

"They're making a conscious choice in what materials they use," Kaufman said. "She wasn't just flying down and getting a piece of grass. They're fully working and getting these fibers." (Ref 10-7)

Both Flood and Kaufman agreed that even if the oriole's craft is instinctual, it takes time and training to perfect it.

Birds demonstrate patience while incubating their eggs. Many go for significant lengths of time without food or water while sitting on eggs to keep them warm and waiting for the eggs to hatch. Different species of birds incubate their eggs for varying lengths of time. Smaller birds incubate for about two weeks, while larger birds have larger eggs and incubate them longer. If the eggs are left uncovered for too long, they become infertile, and more susceptible to predation.

The female Snowy Owl exhibits a great deal of patience while she waits for her mate to bring food to the nest for herself and for their siblings.

Indeed, Snowy Owls are masters at patiently sitting. Photographer Joe Gliozzo comments that "Snowy Owls can sit for very long periods of time without any signs of movement. A Snowy Owl can sit for hours without moving; resting and preserving energy – then in a second it is gone.... I've observed Snowy Owls sitting in one place for more than six hours numerous times. It can get boring, but it's the kind of boring I sure don't mind." (Ref 10-8)

The life of a Wandering Albatross chick is all about patience. After it hatches, the chick spends nine months sitting alone at its nest, most of the time quietly contemplating its surroundings. It has no siblings. The chick's parents are far away, soaring over distant oceans looking for food. They only occasionally return to the nest to quickly deliver a meal before leaving again.

One day, the young albatross stretches its wings and, without any guidance from its parents, leaves for the sea, where it will spend the next six years on the windswept southern oceans before returning to land.

In her poem *Patience Taught by Nature*, Elizabeth Barrett Browning describes her desire to copy the example of the patience found in nature. [Ref 10-9] While humans complain of their lot in life, of all the things that have gone wrong or their future prospects, the birds continue to sing and are untouched by peoples' perceived dreariness of life. Nature is patient and ignorant of human angst. Elizabeth Browning wants to stop feeling the desire for things she does not have, does not need, or cannot have.

> "O Dreary life!" we cry, "O dreary life!"
> And still the generations of the birds
> Sing through our sighing, and the flocks and herds
> Serenely live while we are keeping strife
> With Heaven's true purpose in us, as a knife
> Against which we may struggle. Ocean girds
> Unslackened the dry land: savannah-swards
> Unweary sweep: hills watch, unworn; and rife
> Meek leaves drop yearly from the forest-trees,
> To show, above, the unwasted stars that pass
> In their old glory. O thou God of old!
> Grant me some smaller grace than comes to *these*;—
> But so much patience, as a blade of grass
> Grows by contented through the heat and cold.

Chapter 11 – Be Curious and Playful

"Joy in the universe, and keen curiosity about it all—that has been my religion."

John Burroughs

"Curiosity is more important than knowledge."

Albert Einstein

"We keep moving forward, opening new doors, and trying new things, because we are curious and curiosity keeps leading us down new paths."

Walt Disney

"The curious are always in some danger. If you are curious, you might never come home."

Jeanette Winterson

"This is the real secret of life – to be completely engaged with what you are doing in the here and now. And instead of calling it work, realize it is play."

Alan Watts

"Every one of the geezers who continues to play a leadership role has one quality of overriding importance: neoteny. The dictionary definition is that neoteny, a zoological term, involves 'the retention of youthful

qualities throughout old age.' It is more than merely retaining a youthful appearance, although that is often part of it. Neoteny is the retention of all those wonderful qualities that we associate with youth: curiosity, playfulness, eagerness, fearlessness, warmth, energy."

Warren G. Bennis (scholar on leadership)

Behavior perceived as curiosity-driven or exploratory in nature is widespread among birds. It is a mechanism that serves in approaching new objects. Curiosity implies a desire to learn. Curiosity teaches birds more about their world, expanding their knowledge of both threats and benefits, and helping them react to the unexpected. Curious birds can be more adaptable and will be more successful when encountering changes in their environment.

A biologist with the Loon Preservation Committee in New Hampshire, who has a lot of experience with loons, made the following comments: [Ref 11-1] "Loons are individuals and have a range of personalities. Some of them have a strong curiosity. I've had some swim right up to me, uninvited, whether I was in a kayak or a 15-foot Boston whaler. There are city loons (e.g. Lake Winnipesaukee) and country loons (e.g. 100 acre ponds a mile or more from any road). City loons will generally tolerantly ignore you unless you get in their face (which we shouldn't). Country loons are apt to be more curious about you, and it depends where they fall in the timid-aggressive continuum.

All loons are incredibly aware of what is happening on their lake. I was monitoring an adult brooding two chicks recently. Mom (it was banded so I knew it was the female) was ignoring all the kayakers paddling up to gawk and she couldn't care less about the motor boats whizzing past. But when a man standing on a surfboard using a long paddle showed up, she went berserk with tremolos before he was within 300 meters of her and the chicks. That got the attention of the male, who was foraging around the point. He swam right up to the man and gave him an incredible yodel-tremolo tongue lashing that didn't let up until the guy was 100 meters past the chicks. Loons just don't like strange things on their lake. Loons are also the first to know (and announce) that eagles (or float planes) are in the neighborhood.

A trick I use when I'm trying to read bands is to "wave" the loon in. A hat or bandana waved vigorously enough to make a flapping noise arouses a loon's curiosity and maybe 50 percent of the time it will approach you. Again, it all depends on the loon's personality and mood." [Ref 11-2]

Curiosity can sometimes be dangerous, as A. C. Bent describes: [Ref 11-3] "Curiosity has cost many a loon his life, for it is an easy matter to toll one within gunshot range by remaining hidden, and waving some conspicuous object. The loon cannot resist the impulse to investigate, unless it is an old bird which has learned by experience. A man partially concealed in grass or underbrush near the shore of a lake will sometimes serve to arouse the curiosity of some old loon who will call up a number of his companions to talk it over. They will then swim around in circles, gradually working in nearer. A sudden movement will cause them to dive like a flash or go scudding away, but they will swim up again, alternately advancing or retreating, until a shot from the man satisfies that curiosity."

The behavior of loons under certain circumstances shows peculiar traits of character. In A. C. Bent's *Life History of North American Diving Birds*, Dr. P. L. Hatch (1892) relates the following earliest dawn performance of a family of loons: [Ref 11-4]

"The night is spent in proximity to each other on the water, somewhat removed from the land. And in the earliest morning, notes of the parent male soon call out a response from the other members of the family, when they all draw near, and after cavorting around each other after the manner of graceful skaters for a brief time, they fall into line, side by side, and lifting their wings simultaneously, they start off in a foot race on the water like a line of school children, running with incredible speed a full quarter of a mile without lowering their wings or pausing an instant, wheel around in a short circle (in which some of them get a little behind) and retrace their course to the place of starting. This race, after but a moment's pause, is repeated over and over again, with unabated zest, until by some undiscoverable signal it ceases as suddenly as it began. Its termination is characterized by a subsequent general congratulation manifested by the medley of loon notes. This walking, or rather running, upon the face of the quiet lake waters is a marvel of pedal performance, so swiftly do the thin, sharp legs move in the race, the wings being continuously held at about half extent. Soon after this is over, the male parent takes to wing to seek his food in some distant part of the same or some other lake, which is soon followed by the departure of the female in another direction, while the young swim away in various directions to seek their supplies nearer the place of nightly rendezvous."

Sometimes, behavior which appears to be done joyfully and in a playful manner, is really an activity that prepares the participants to survive better in the future. Loons need to patter along the surface of a lake for a long time before they can become airborne. Their legs are positioned far to the rear in their bodies and their bones are heavier than those of most birds, enabling them to dive and to remain underwater. The seemingly playful activity among the adult loons and their offspring described above is undoubtedly intended to strengthen the leg muscles of the young birds, so that they will be better prepared to take off in flight from the lake.

A. C. Bent comments on the difficulty that loons have walking on land as follows: [Ref 11-5] "I believe that they usually sleep on the water, but when it is safe to do so they often come ashore to sleep. I have several times surprised one well up on a sandy beach, where it had been spending the night or had gone ashore to dry and sand its plumage. Its attempts to regain the water were more precipitous than graceful, as it scrambled or stumbled down the beach, falling on its breast at every few yards, darting its head and neck about, humping its back and straining every muscle to make speed."

FIGURE 11-1 - LOONS swimming in San Francisco Bay. Photo by the author.

FIGURE 11-2 – LOON with its eyes below the water searching for food. Photo by the author.

FIGURE 11-3 – LOON in San Francisco Bay with Alcatraz in the background. Photo by the author.

Sometimes, activities that birds engage in seem to have no other prime function than to elicit pleasure. To an observer, they seem to enjoy playing. However, often their playfulness is a serious business that increases their physical and cognitive abilities, preparing them to survive and have better future lives. Just as playing games and using their imagination are vital in the development of children, so the actions of birds who appear to be playing are important in their ability to cope in the world. Nevertheless, these playful activities can still be enjoyed by both children and birds.

Ravens are extremely intelligent birds and are playful creatures. They are acrobats in the sky, where they "surf updrafts, fly upside down, and even turn somersaults, just because they can. Young ravens have been seen playing a fun game of catch by dropping a stick while in flight and then quickly swooping to catch it before it hits the ground." (Ref 11-6)

FIGURE 11-4 - THE COMMON Raven is a large, black majestic bird. Courtesy of Lee Karney, USFWS.

The extent of play and how much play each bird species carries into maturity varies. Different birds engage in different types of play to help them develop a range of skills. All the types of play that wild birds use help them to develop necessary survival skills. Even adult birds may continue to play and refine their abilities, though not necessarily with the same frequency as juvenile birds play. [Ref 11-7]

Three types of play are recognized among birds: Solo or solitary locomotory play is when individual birds enjoy their own company and engage in activities such as "running, skipping, jumping, ducking, rolling, hanging, swinging, dancing and even sliding and snow-romping". Locomotor play includes all types of flight-related play such as aerial acrobatics, including hanging and flying upside down. Object play is when an individual plays with different objects. It can involve the close inspection of objects to learn about their structure, how they work, and if they are edible. Social play occurs when two or more individuals play. [Ref 11-8]

Although birds generally have less leisure time than humans in which to engage in play, they may sometimes play because it is a pleasurable experience. Although these possibilities are little researched, playing may reduce stress, aid social bonding, or just be pleasurable.

Chapter 12 – Be Creative and Innovative

"Creativity involves breaking out of established patterns in order to look at things in a different way."

Edward de Bono

"Learning and innovation go hand in hand. The arrogance of success is to think that what you did yesterday will be sufficient for tomorrow."

William Pollard

"An inventor is simply a person who doesn't take his education too seriously. You see, from the time a person is six years old until he graduates from college, he has to take three or four examinations a year. If he flunks once, he is out. But an inventor is almost always failing. He tries and fails maybe a thousand times. If he succeeds once then he's in. These two things are diametrically opposite. We often say that the biggest job we have is to teach a newly-hired employee how to fail intelligently. We have to train him to experiment over and over and to keep on trying and failing until he learns what will work."

Charles Kettering

"We all operate in two contrasting modes, which might be called open and closed. The open mode is more relaxed, more receptive, more exploratory, more democratic, more playful and more humorous. The closed mode is the tighter, more rigid, more hierarchical, more tunnel-visioned.

The closed mode can be helpful. If you are leaping a ravine, the moment of takeoff is a bad time for considering alternative strategies.... Do it in the closed mode. But the moment the action is over, try to return to the 'open' mode – to open your mind again to all the feedback from our action that enables us to tell whether the action has been successful, or whether further action is needed to improve on what we have done. In other words, we must return to the open mode, because in that mode we are the most aware, most receptive, most creative, and therefore at our most intelligent."

John Cleese

Birds employ creativity and innovation in novel ways to obtain food, and in new ways to communicate. They innovate when they have to respond to new problems they have never encountered before.

In a rapidly changing world, extinction is a real risk for a variety of bird species. Behavioral innovativeness can sometimes help to reduce this risk, by allowing birds to cope as their native habitats are altered or destroyed. On the other hand, poorly innovative species are particularly sensitive to habitat destruction and deserve special attention from conservationists in order to survive current environmental changes.

Creativity seems to be most highly developed in birds who are generalists, who have varied food sources, who frequently expose themselves to novel or unusual conditions, and who have relatively long lives.

Several examples of birds inventing new ways to obtain food follow.

At the beginning of the 20th century milk used to be delivered to British doorsteps in bottles that had no tops and birds had easy access to the fat rich cream that settled at the top of the bottle. However, after World War One, the bottles became sealed with aluminum foil bottle tops to keep the milk fresher. Then, Blue Tits in the United Kingdom learned how to pierce the bottle tops to reach the cream they were after. With the introduction of semi-skimmed and skimmed milk and the decrease of milk deliveries to houses, this phenomenon has now practically died out.

In a town in western India, temple caretakers fill small cups with clarified butter to fuel lanterns for prayer. The Rufous Treepie, a member of the crow family, has learned to fly into the temple, grab the lit candles, and carry them away. They then remove the wick – which is still on fire – shake it until extinguished, and eat the wick and cup of butter. [Ref 12-1]

Gulls are known for dropping crabs onto hard rocks or pavements to break the outer shell. Many birds will soak hard food items in water to soften them. Egrets are known to drop insects and bits of bread into the water as bait for fish. Crows will drop walnuts on roads where cars can drive over them and crack the nuts open. These examples are some of the solutions birds have invented in order to obtain food.

The author witnessed the following example of a female Brewer's Blackbird using her creativity to look for food:

<u>*Brewer's Blackbird*</u>

Standing outside the Warming Hut, I watched a female Brewer's Blackbird enter through the door of the Warming Hut. As I was curious, I followed her inside to see where she would go and how she would get out again. This Brewer's Blackbird seemed to know exactly where she was going. She turned left after the entrance and continued walking another 20 feet to where there are indoor tables and chairs to accommodate people who have bought some food and drink at the counter. She walked around the tables and chairs for some time looking for crumbs, and then turned around and retraced her steps, turning the corner to go out the door of the Warming Hut. This seemed like a regular routine she followed.

FIGURE 12-1 - THE WARMING Hut. Photo by the author.

Some birds employ creativity in the creation of their songs and in ways to communicate. Humans do not consider birds' singing as unusual. But the ability to sing is actually quite rare in evolutionary terms. Many animals can make sounds, but few in the same way birds do. Also, only a small subset of animals is capable of learning vocalizations when they're young by imitating other members of their species. This puts songbirds in very rarified territory along with humans, dolphins, whales, and elephants. [Ref 12-2]

Why is some bird song so complex? "I haven't heard a reasonable explanation of why birdsong is so complicated," says Jeff Markowitz, a graduate student in computational neuroscience at Boston University. [Ref 12-3]

Are the singers trying to create the most beautiful songs they can? Scientists are trying to understand the complexity of bird song. The complex songs of canaries contain extremely flexible phrases. Scientists may find unnecessary components of canary song—embellishments that don't help or perhaps even hinder a male bird in his quest to find a mate. By removing parts of the song that researchers suspect aren't important, they could see how the females behave in response. If females react the same to a simplified song as they do to a full song, it's possible that the additional notes are the male canary's just playing around and being creative. "I think with the right tools, you can start to look at birds like the Nightingale, the Brown Thrasher, and other wild, complex singers," says Markowitz. "We may find that all of this complexity serves absolutely no purpose." (Ref 12-4)

The Northern Mockingbird (*Mimus polyglottos*) is a talented mimic who is able to exactly reproduce the songs of other species, switching from one distinct tune to another with great ease. Mockingbirds have even been reported to imitate bells, sirens, whistles, and other sounds they hear. The eighteenth-century naturalist Mark Catesby wrote the following description of the Northern Mockingbird in 1731: (Ref 12-5) "Hernandez justly calls it the queen of all singing birds. The Indians, by way of eminence or admiration, call it *Cencontlatolly* or four hundred tongues; and we call it the mock-bird, from its wonderful mocking and imitating the notes of all birds, from the hummingbird to the eagle."

Some birds use creativity in the construction of their nests. Dr. Henry William Smith and his wife Felicia documented the birds around their Connecticut nature area. They served food to the various migrating birds and began to provide yarns in various colors at the start of the nesting season. They wanted to see if the birds, and especially the orioles who wove elaborate nests, would be interested in using these yarns to build their nests. They discovered that individual female orioles and other birds used these colorful yarns to fabricate elaborate nests. Different females chose different colors, with some preferring white yarns, while others selected other colors.

Dr. Smith wrote: (Ref 12-6) "The net result was that these nests of 1931, collectively, made up the most spectacular exhibit ever seen in our treetops. It was a great show. In early June, within a hundred yards of the house, you could see:

(a) four nests of the Baltimore oriole, made of pure white yarn, with or without scarlet trimmings;

(b) five robins' nests decorated with masses of red, white, orange and blue yarn;

(c) two kingbirds' nests, one red and white, the other blue and white with red and orange trimmings;

(d) two catbirds' nests decorated with orange yarn;

(e) nests of redstart and least flycatcher and yellow warbler made almost exclusively of white cotton;

(f) three cedar waxwings' nests, one decorated with orange, the second resplendent in red, and a third a gigantic cradle of yarn in spectrum yellow, blue, lavender, white and red."

Surprisingly, although these colorful nests stood out against the green leaves, predators avoided them, as they looked like such alien structures.

"No one can prove that the robins do not understand that these bright decorations are alarming to jays and crows, and therefore safeguard their nests. Nor can anyone prove that they do not have a decorative sense, and select the yarns for their sheer beauty." [Ref 12-7]

"These are remarkable testimonials to the powers of imagination, the teachableness, the mobility of mind and retentiveness of memory of our 'educated' birds. A creature that possesses such qualities of mind is far from being a mere automaton." [Ref 12-8]

Chapter 13 – Use Your Intelligence

"It is better to have a fair intellect that is well used than a powerful one that is idle."

Bryant H. McGill

"Intelligence is what you use when you don't know what to do: when neither innateness nor learning has prepared you for the particular situation."

Jean Piaget

"The true sign of intelligence is not knowledge but imagination."

Albert Einstein

"When I see a dolphin, I know it's just as smart as I am."

Captain Beefheart

"These little grey cells. It is up to them."

Agatha Christie

Humans find it difficult to acknowledge the intelligence of other species because historically intelligence has been seen as a quality that sets primates, and especially humans, apart. However, the intelligence of species besides humans is readily demonstrated through their conscious actions.

Intelligence is the ability to understand and think about things, and to gain and use knowledge, instead of doing things automatically or by instinct. At its broadest, intelligence refers to the functioning of a number of related faculties and abilities that enable the individual to adapt and respond to environmental pressures.

Ludlow Griscom distinguished between instinct and intelligence as follows: [Ref 13-1] "Instinct is the inherited capacity or propensity to perform seemingly rational acts without conscious design or instruction. Intelligence is quickness of understanding as distinct from perception, the power of reasoning, drawing an inference, or working out advantageous conduct under difficult or novel conditions."

Scientists have argued for decades over whether wild creatures, including birds, show genuine intelligence. The cognitive abilities of birds have been documented in numerous experiments. Studies found that birds could manufacture and use tools, use insight to solve problems, make inferences about cause-effect relationships, recognize themselves in a mirror, and plan for future needs, among other cognitive skills previously considered possible only by primates.

Intelligence is not limited to those birds who are thought to be very smart, such as crows, ravens, and jays. In experiments at Cardiff University in Britain [Ref 13-2], a pigeon identified subtle differences between abstract designs. It could tell that a Picasso was not the same as a Monet. The experiment seemed to show that pigeons can hold concepts or ideas – in this case Picasso's painting style – in their heads.

Recent research has suggested that California Scrub-Jays, along with several other corvids, are among the most intelligent of animals. The brain-to-body mass ratio of adult Scrub-Jays rivals that of chimpanzees and cetaceans, and is dwarfed only by that of humans. Studies have shown that they can remember locations of over 200 food caches, as well as the food item in each cache and its rate of decay. [Ref 13-3]

To protect their caches from pilfering conspecifics, Scrub-Jays will choose locations out of sight of their competitors, or will re-cache them once they are alone, suggesting that they can take into account the perspective of others. [Ref 13-4]

The definition of sagacity is keenness of discernment or judgement. If you are wise and prone to evaluating information before making a decision, you possess sagacity, the trait of solid judgment and intelligent choices.

A.C. Bent describes the wisdom of Black-bellied Plovers as follows: [Ref 13-5] "These plovers, no longer black bellied now, spend the winter in the southern United States and from there southward to central Brazil and Peru.... I have seen them in immense flocks on the great mud flats among the Florida keys and we had them with us all winter on the beaches and sandy islands about Tampa Bay. They showed their sagacity by their confiding tameness on the protected bathing beaches and by their extreme wildness on the outer islands, where it was almost impossible to approach them within gunshot range."

Until recently, the long-held belief about the structure of the avian brain could not be reconciled with demonstrations of birds' sophisticated cognitive abilities. Recent research and advances in knowledge suggest that birds, who are separated from mammals by over 300 million years of independent evolution, have developed brains capable of primate-like consciousness through a process of convergent evolution.

Similarity in traits can occur in two ways. Both species may have acquired the trait by descent from a common ancestor. In this case, the structures are homologous. On the other hand, the structures may be independent adaptations to similar conditions in their habitat. In this case the structures are analogous. Analogous structures evolved to do the same job, not because they were inherited from a common ancestor. Convergent evolution leads to analogous features. It is the development of similar structures in distantly related organisms because of adapting to similar environments or strategies of life.

Convergent evolution is when different organisms independently evolve similar traits. This happens because they live in similar habitats, and have to develop solutions to the same kinds of problems.

William Thorpe, who was the leading authority on bird learning in his time, stated in his 1963 book *Learning and Instinct in Animals*: [Ref 13-6] "The poor development in birds of any brain structure corresponding to the cerebral cortex of mammals led to the assumption among neurologists not only that birds are primarily creatures of instinct, but also that they are very little endowed with the ability to learn. There is no doubt that this preconceived notion, based on a misconceived view of brain mechanisms, hindered the development of experimental studies of bird learning."

The study of avian intelligence has witnessed dramatic advances. The avian brain structure was misjudged in the past. The forebrain, which also produced the mammalian neocortex, derives from the pallium. The basic function of the pallium is to serve as a linkage between sensory inputs and motor outputs. It serves as an interface between sensory and perceptual processing and mechanisms which modulate behavior. This is also the basic function of the mammalian cortex.

Erich Jarvis et al in a 2005 paper *Avian brains and a new understanding of vertebrate brain evolution* [Ref 13-7] stated that studies demonstrate that so-called 'primitive' regions of avian brains are actually sophisticated processing regions similar to those in mammals. These regions carry out sensory processing, motor control, and sensorimotor learning just as is done in the mammalian neocortex. "We have to get rid of the idea that mammals – and humans in particular – are the pinnacle of evolution. We also have to understand that evolution is not linear, but an intricate branching process. So, we can't automatically expect to track a structure in the human brain back to other current vertebrate species....Evolution has created more than one way to generate complex behavior – the mammal way and the bird way. And they're comparable to one another. In fact, some birds have evolved cognitive abilities that are far more complex than in many mammals."

Bret Stretka in *Bird Brains Are Far More Humanlike Than Once Thought* [Ref 13-8] commented that it was assumed that the avian brain was limited in function because it lacked a neocortex. In mammals, the neocortex is the outer layer of the brain that allows for complex cognition and creativity, and that makes up most of what, in vertebrates as a whole, is called the pallium. New findings show that birds have a brain structure comparable to the neocortex, but taking a different shape. At the cellular level, the brain region is laid out much like the mammalian cortex.

Vanderbilt University neuroscientist Suzana Herculano-Houzel wrote that the whole of the pallium in mammals and birds has similar development origins and connectivity, and therefore [the pallia of both classes] should be considered equivalent structures.

Martin Stacho et al in *A cortex-like canonical circuit in the avian forebrain* (Ref 13-9) establish that the bird pallium has similar organization to the mammalian cortex. "Although birds lack a cerebral cortex, they do have a pallium, and this is considered to be analogous, if not homologous, to the cerebral cortex." An outstanding feature of the mammalian cortex is its layered architecture. In a detailed anatomical study of the bird pallium, Stacho describes a similarly layered architecture. Despite the nuclear organization of the bird pallium, it has an organization like that of the mammalian cortex.

For over 100 years, the avian forebrain has been a riddle for neuroscientists. Birds demonstrate exceptional cognitive abilities comparable to those of mammals, but their forebrain organization is very different. The findings suggest that likely an ancient microcircuit that existed in the last common stem amniote might have been evolutionarily conserved and partly modified in birds and mammals. The avian version of this blueprint could possibly generate properties similar to the neocortex and thus provide a neurobiological explanation for the comparable outstanding perceptual and cognitive abilities of both birds and mammals.

Because their neurons are smaller, the pallium of songbirds and parrots actually comprises many more information-processing neuronal units than the equivalent-sized mammalian cortices. In a 2016 research article (Ref 13-10), scientists stated that "the brains of parrots and songbirds contain on average twice as many neurons as primate brains of the same mass, indicating that avian brains have higher neuron packing densities than mammalian brains. Thus, large-brained parrots and corvids have forebrain neuron counts equal to or greater than primates with much larger brains."

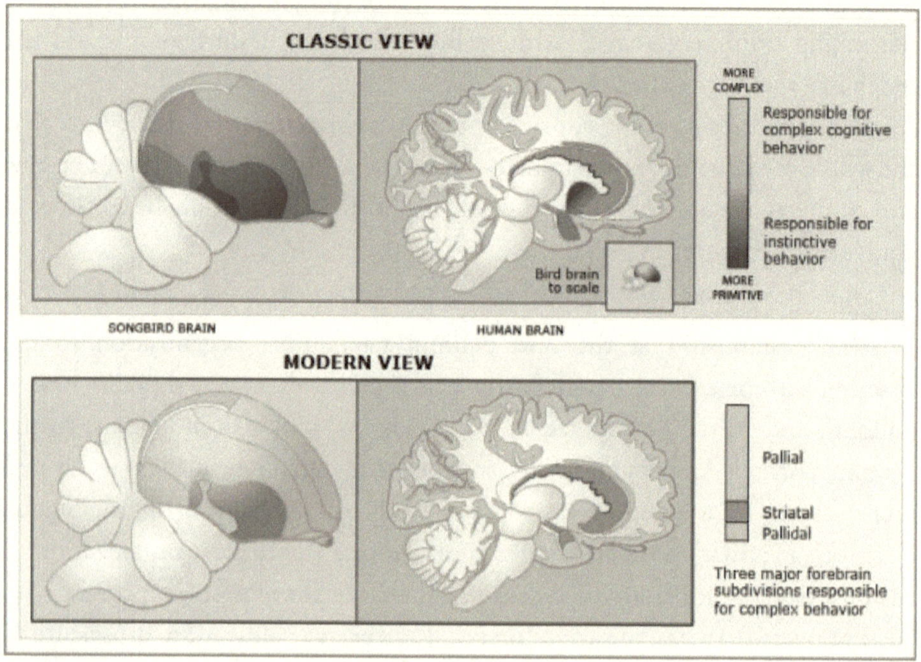

FIGURE 13-1 - COMPARISON of the classic and the modern views of songbird and human brains. Image credit: Zina Deretsky, National Science Foundation.

A wide range of studies have recently demonstrated that the so-called "primitive" regions of avian brains are actually sophisticated processing regions homologous to those in mammals. The above illustrations compare the traditional view of the primitive avian brain as a subregion of the human brain with the new view that the avian brain has subregions proportional to those in humans. Scientists now know that the complexities of avian brain regions allow sensory processing, motor control and sensorimotor learning as in the mammalian neocortex. [Ref 13-11]

Chapter 14 – Show Loyalty

"Loyalty and friendship, which is to me the same, created all the wealth that I've ever thought I'd have."

Ernie Banks

"You don't earn loyalty in a day. You earn loyalty day-by-day."

Jeffrey Gitomer

"....it isn't things and proximity, or even blood that holds us all together. What makes a family is love and loyalty."

Genevieve Dewey

"Things are never quite as scary when you've got a best friend."

Bill Watterson

"The only way to have a friend is to be one."

Ralph Waldo Emerson

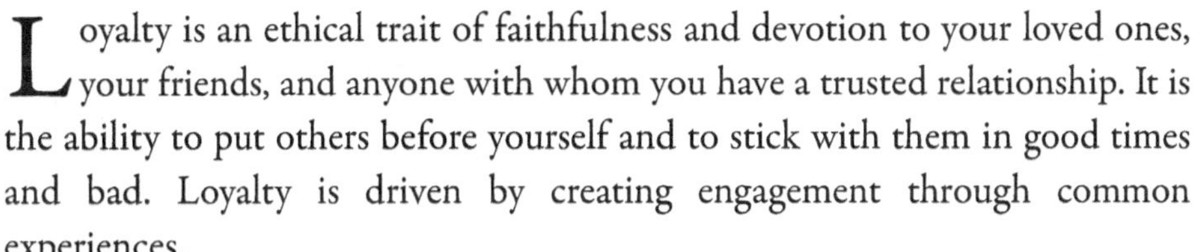

Loyalty is an ethical trait of faithfulness and devotion to your loved ones, your friends, and anyone with whom you have a trusted relationship. It is the ability to put others before yourself and to stick with them in good times and bad. Loyalty is driven by creating engagement through common experiences.

Among the most loyal of bird species are the storks, geese, and swans, who stay together night and day during the whole year, even when they travel on migration. But there are many bird species that form long term, strong pair bonds that could be defined as mating for life. While any of these individual birds may seek a new mate if the pair cannot produce eggs or if one partner is injured or dies, some familiar bird species that are considered life partners include the following: Atlantic Puffins, Bald Eagles, Barn Owls, Bewick's Swans, Black-billed Magpies, Black Vultures, Blue Jays, California Condors, Canada Geese, Common Ravens, Golden Eagles, Gyrfalcons, Laysan Albatrosses, Long-billed Curlews, Macaroni Penguins, Mute Swans, Oak Titmice, Ospreys, Pileated Woodpeckers, Red-tailed Hawks, Sandhill Cranes, Scarlet Macaws, Snow Geese, Wrentits, and Whooping Cranes. [Ref 14-1]

Bald Eagles mate for life unless one of the two dies. Their spectacular courtship rituals involve the birds' locking talons, then flipping, spinning, and twirling through the air in a maneuver called a Cartwheel Display. They break apart seemingly at the last moment, just before hitting the ground. [Ref 14-2]

Laysan Albatrosses, which don't breed until they're eight or nine years old, are monogamous, annually solidifying their bond through ritual dancing. "If they do lose their mate, they will go through a year or two of a mourning period," says John Klavitter, U.S. Fish and Wildlife Service biologist at Midway Atoll. "After that, they will do a courtship dance to try to find another mate." (Ref 14-3)

The Wandering Albatross returns to its home island in the sub-Antarctic and Antarctic at about six years of age for the sole purpose of finding a mate. Other albatrosses are there, and they begin to dance. It can take years of dancing to pick a mate. A Wandering Albatross might be 15 years old by the time it nests for the first time. From then on, it will generally stick faithfully with its mate until one dies, which might not be for decades as these large birds typically live for 50 years. At sea, pairs don't stay together, as it is too easy to get separated over the open ocean. Pairs would have to spend too much energy keeping track of each other's whereabouts. The birds make the most of their limited time together at the nest, and often sleep with the head of one bird against the breast of its mate.

Scarlet Macaws spend their lives together. They preen each other and their young, picking bugs from their feathers. Scarlet Macaw parents, which reach sexual maturity sometime between age three and four, won't raise new chicks until their previous ones have fledged and are independent. (Ref 14-4)

Whooping Cranes—who are monogamous and mate for life—bow their heads, flap their wings, leap and bounce off stiffened legs in the effort to secure a partner. This pairing off usually happens when the birds are between two and three years old. (Ref 14-5)

Atlantic Puffins don't breed until they're between three and six years old. Once they do, they keep their partners, returning to the same burrow each season, sharing egg-incubating and parenting duties, and performing what's known as billing, during which the birds rub their beaks together. (Ref 14-6)

About 90 percent of bird species are socially monogamous, meaning a male and a female form a pair bond. But monogamy does not necessarily mean that they mate for life. A pair bond may last for just one nesting, for one breeding season, for several seasons, or for life.

It is estimated that up to 70 percent of birds may form long-term pair bonds, meaning that they stay together year after year. In some cases, they go their separate ways after the breeding season, and then come back together in the next mating season.

Male and female sharing of parental duties varies among bird species. Having two parents sharing incubation and feeding duties greatly increases the chances of raising healthy young and avoiding predation when the nest is left unguarded.

Some larger birds who mate for life may do so for practical reasons. Many larger birds produce only one brood of chicks a year and the offspring take longer to incubate and grow. Mated pairs who stay together are ready to breed earlier in the season and therefore have more time to raise their young. The more broods the pair raise together, the better they become at looking after them, so the chicks are more likely to survive. Finding a mate takes a lot of time and energy. Large migratory birds like geese and swans prefer to stay with one partner and keep their strength for their long journeys. (Ref 14-7)

Mated birds may protect one another, share food resources, or do other things to show their affection and caring. They may display their bond with each other through mutual preening or allopreening, which consists of birds gently nibbling each other's head and neck feathers – areas that are hard for a bird to reach. Also, birds may simply perch closely next to each other, sometimes leaning somewhat on their mate.

Although it is debatable whether behaviors that might be considered emotional are really instinctual, birds do show affection and loyalty to their mates, their families, and even to their friends. Birds that mate for life may show love toward one another in many ways, including sharing companionship throughout the year. Parent birds are caring toward their hatchlings, which may be a demonstration of parental love. While these emotions may not last beyond one breeding season or brood, they are still strong attachments.

"There are a few species of birds that meet, court and form pair bonds that result in many offspring, year after year, until one of the pair dies. For nearly all swans, geese, ducks, cranes, storks and a few others, long-term monogamy is the preferred relationship. Even though these birds are quite loyal, few demonstrate the fidelity of the Bewick's swan, a European native. At the Wildfowl Trust in Slimbridge, England, swans have been studied for more than 50 years." (Ref 14-8)

The Wildfowl & Wetlands Trust (WWT) at Slimbridge was set up in 1946 as a center for science and conservation. Its founder, Sir Peter Scott (1909-1989), was a British ornithologist, conservationist, painter, naval officer, and broadcaster. He took practical steps to prevent the extinction of species by protecting natural areas and increasing public awareness. He is widely remembered as one of the fathers of modern conservation. Scott traveled to most of the countries of the world promoting conservation on every continent. In 1961 he helped found the World Wildlife Fund (WWF) and he designed its panda logo. He was Honorary Chairman of the WWF International Council. In 1973 Peter Scott was the first person ever to be knighted for services to conservation.

David Attenborough said about Sir Peter Scott: "Long before words like biodiversity were coined, Peter looked out from that huge window in his house at Slimbridge and realized our lives are so linked with our natural world that we have to learn to love it and look after it." (Ref 14-9)

FIGURE 14-1 – *Taking to Wing* by Sir Peter Scott.

Peter Scott dedicated much of his time at Slimbridge to watching and studying Bewick's swans. He was the first person to notice that each bird has a unique bill pattern, thus making it possible to identify individuals. The conservation team at the Wildfowl & Wetlands Trust used this technique to identify and record individual Bewick's swans for more than 50 years, one of the longest single species research studies. Over that time, more than 4,000 swans were recorded.

The study found that Bewick's swans have loyal partners for life. There were only two instances of 'divorce' among the swans studied.

Paired birds seek out each other if separated during migration, and perform joyous ceremonies when they are reunited. They mourn following the loss of a mate, generally taking at least a year to re-pair, and longer to breed with a new partner. The swans also form strong extended family bonds. When parents, offspring, and siblings come together at feeding sites and on the roost, they honk a soft greeting.

Bewick's swans are migratory, breeding in northern Russia and wintering in the United Kingdom. They travel approximately 2,500 km (1,600 miles) between breeding and wintering sites. They migrate in their family groups, with the parents adapting their pace to that of their cygnets, some of whom are only three months old at the start of the migration. This means that families often arrive at their final overwintering home later than pairs and single birds.

Bewick's swans tend to be long-lived, but usually only two or three cygnets per family make it to their wintering sites in northwest Europe, and less than half of the population makes a breeding attempt each year. The number of Northwest European Bewick's swans has dropped by a third in recent years and there are estimated to be fewer than 21,000 left.

Every autumn, Bewick's swans face a dangerous migration to the United Kingdom from northern Russia. Along the route between their breeding and wintering sites there are predators, fewer wetlands, and the risk of hitting power lines. In spring, they do it all again as they fly back to Russia. They are probably negatively affected by the rapidly changing climate of the Arctic. They are illegally hunted – often mistakenly because their small size makes them resemble geese in low winter light. They are also susceptible to eating the lead ammunition from shotguns, which poisons, weakens, and often kills them.

The Bewick's swan news from Slimbridge for the winter of 2021 was as follows: [Ref 14-10] "The beginning of December brought about the first 'swanfall' after a steady start to Bewick's season. Overnight on 30th November, 26 majestic Bewick's swans arrived, after completing the final leg of their autumn migration. Encouraged by the onset of winter conditions at their breeding grounds in Arctic Russia, the Bewick's swans began their journey back in September and have since been enjoying the comforts and plentiful feeding opportunities at wetlands across Estonia, Latvia and Lithuania. Hence the initial slow start to the Bewick's swan season at Slimbridge.

The appearance of so many swans is called a 'swanfall', and marks the final stage of their epic journey from Arctic Russia to the comparatively warmer weather of the United Kingdom. This year's first 'swanfall' came almost a month after the first pair touched down at Slimbridge on 5th November.

The 'swanfall' saw the exciting arrival of Slimbridge regular Maisie, named after Reserve Warden, Martin McGill's, daughter. Maisie arrived this year with her partner Mayfeld and their first two cygnets. At just three months old, these cygnets have completed their first 2,500 km migration. Maisie first wintered at Slimbridge in 2014-15 where she was fitted with a GPS collar, and for a few years the Wildfowl & Wetlands Trust was able to track her movements. Unfortunately during migration Maisie somehow lost the tracking collar. Maisie has been with Mayfeld since the winter of 2016-17 but this is the first time they have brought cygnets to Slimbridge (pictured below).

FIGURE 14-2 – BEWICK'S Swans at the Wildfowl & Wetlands Trust (1)

Tracked swan Arkadi (pictured below) has also been spotted on site. Arkadi has brought back 5 cygnets in his time with previous mate Crete, however Crete did not return in the winter 2016-2017. Arkadi has returned this year with a new mate, Kritsa.

FIGURE 14-3 – BEWICK'S Swans at the Wildfowl & Wetlands Trust (2) https://www.wwt.org.uk/wetland-centres/slimbridge/news/swan-news# Seventy-one Bewick's Swans remained on site on 3 January 2021."

Chapter 15 – Accept Reality

"Life is a series of natural and spontaneous changes. Don't resist them; that only creates sorrow. Let reality be reality. Let things flow naturally forward in whatever way they like."

Lao Tzu

"Accept – then act. Whatever the present moment contains, accept it as if you had chosen it. Always work with it, not against it.... This will miraculously transform your whole life."

Eckhart Tolle

Accepting the reality of a situation brings peace and an ability to go forward with what needs to be done. Following are two examples of birds who first realized and then accepted their situations, and who made the best decisions they could considering what had happened to them.

The first example of a Western Willet was witnessed by the author:

<u>*Western Willet*</u>

On the morning of December 9, 2018, I sat on the top step of a stairway leading down to Marshall's Beach on the west side of the Golden Gate Bridge in San Francisco. Here I often watched and photographed the shorebirds foraging on the beach. A lone Western Willet flew onto the beach, flashing its white underwing coverts. When it ran after an outgoing wave, it limped and favored one leg. It was lame and had difficulty trying to run after a retreating wave and then getting out of the way of the incoming water. I wondered how it was going to survive—however, it could still fly.

Then it did something strange. It hobbled along the beach closer and closer to where I sat, finally taking shelter behind a rock right below me. I could just see its head projecting from the rock. It appeared to be watching me. What was it doing? Was it trying to find a safe place to hide and rest? It stayed there for about fifteen minutes while I sat very still, not even daring to move to take its picture.

The tide was coming in and the incoming waves spread further up onto the beach, encroaching behind the rock where the Willet rested. It was forced to move away from the shelter of the rock and it limped onto the beach. Here it started to follow a retreating wave and then tried hurrying back up the beach to avoid getting wet. Sometimes it had to fly to avoid the incoming water as it wasn't able to walk quickly enough. It then moved further along the beach and joined a group of Sanderlings. I felt a great respect for this Western Willet who courageously did its very best to survive.

The second example of a bird who first realized and then accepted its current situation is a mother Snowy Owl.

Snowy Owls are nomadic birds that nest in different areas in different years depending on where their prey species, primarily lemmings, are more abundant. Within a particular area in their breeding range, they will breed every three to nine years, moving elsewhere in-between before returning again. [Ref 15-2] In years when their preferred food of lemmings is hard to find, Snowy Owls will either not nest at all, or will have smaller clutches.

Baby Snowy Owls are not all born at the same time in the nest. The nestling from the last-laid egg is therefore smaller than the others and may be considered the runt of the litter. Smaller chicks will crawl under larger chicks, apparently for warmth. Some newly hatched chicks may lose up to 45 percent of their body mass, while other chicks gain mass daily [Ref 15-2]

The earlier-hatched chicks are not aggressive towards the younger, smaller chicks and the female Snowy Owl feeds all the chicks, although the older ones are usually fed first. Nestlings depart the nest on foot, flightless, at about three weeks of age. Before then, chicks can be out of the nest bowl, but still remain on the nest mound one or two meters from the bowl. Once out of the nest, chicks still depend on their parents for food and protection from predators, and they must withstand the environmental conditions in the far north, including wind, cold, and rain. In extreme weather, they will huddle under their mother's wings. Some chicks die in the nest and the main causes of nestling mortality are usually starvation and chilling.

The Public Broadcasting System's *Nature: Magic of the Snowy Owl* [Ref 15-3] followed a breeding Snowy Owl family in a year when lemmings were scarce and hard to find. There were four young Snowies in the nest. The most recently-born owlet was noticeably smaller than its three older siblings. When the father brought a lemming and gave it to the mother to feed to the young, the smallest chick was not as quick to rush toward its mother. The youngest, smallest owlet was unintentionally crowded out by the older siblings who crowded about their mother, eager for a meal.

Lemmings were scarce that year in the vicinity of the nest and the father owl's deliveries were far apart and insufficient to satisfy the hunger of the nestlings and their mother. The mother owl tried to apportion the available food equally, but she was far-sighted, and although her distance vision was excellent, she did not see as well close-up, and was not able to apportion food equally among her young.

When the three older owlets were three weeks old, they walked a short distance away from the nest bowl. These young Snowies still had the downy feathers of nestlings, which didn't keep them very warm or dry. By this time, the fourth youngest Snowy Owl was so much smaller and more vulnerable to the cold than its older siblings, who tried to keep the smallest owlet warm by gathering around it. But when the older owlets wandered a short distance away, the youngest owlet was becoming too weak to follow them and it was left sitting apart from them. The mother Snowy Owl noticed this and realized that her youngest owlet was suffering. She went over to her sibling and put her wing over it to protect it from the cold and to keep it warm. In this manner, she continued to brood the littlest owlet.

But the youngest Snowy was too weak to survive, and it succumbed. The mother gently tried to revive it over and over again, but she eventually acknowledged that it was lifeless and that it had died.

The mother Snowy Owl was suffering from extreme hunger, as were her chicks, due to the inability of the father owl to locate and bring back sufficient prey to the nest site. In order to save her other chicks, she had to give them sustenance. She finally accepted the reality of her loss and decided that she needed to try to save the lives of her remaining siblings. She saved their lives by giving them her youngest owlet, who had left this world.

In Robert Frost's poem *Acceptance*, Frost observes that when the sun sets and darkness falls, there is absolute acceptance by the birds and by all of Nature. (Ref 15-4)

> When the spent sun throws up its rays on cloud
> And goes down burning into the gulf below,
> No voice in nature is heard to cry aloud
> At what has happened. Birds, at least must know
> It is the change to darkness in the sky.
> Murmuring something quiet in her breast,
> One bird begins to close a faded eye;
> Or overtaken too far from his nest,
> Hurrying low above the grove, some waif
> Swoops just in time to his remembered tree.
> At most he thinks or twitters softly, 'Safe!'
> Now let the night be dark for all of me.
> Let the night be too dark for me to see
> Into the future. Let what will be, be.

Chapter 16 – Show Resilience After a Setback

"Resilience is accepting your new reality, even if it's less good than the one you had before. You can fight it, you can do nothing but scream about what you've lost, or you can accept that and try to put together something that's good."

Elizabeth Edwards

"Resilience isn't a single skill. It's a variety of skills and coping mechanisms. To bounce back from bumps in the road as well as failures, you should focus on emphasizing the positive."

Jean Chatzky

"Resilience is knowing that you are the only one that has the power and responsibility to pick yourself up."

Mary Holloway

"Resilience is very different from being numb. Resilience means you experience, you feel, you fail, you hurt. You fall. But, you keep going."

Yasmin Mogahed

"Birds sing after a storm; why shouldn't people feel as free to delight in whatever sunlight remains to them?"

Rose Kennedy

Resilience is the capability of withstanding shock without permanent deformation or rupture. It is the tendency to recover from misfortune or change. Birds are resilient and will come back when given a chance.

House Sparrows

The author frequently walked along a street near Fisherman's Wharf when she lived in San Francisco. A row of deciduous trees lined the sidewalk of this street. House Sparrows gathered together in the tree on the corner and were always noisily chirping. The author named this tree "The Singing Tree". One day, the street was noticeably quiet. The sparrows' tree had been cut down. All that remained was the stump. The author wondered where would the sparrows go now? Would they search for and find some new tree where they would all gather together to chirp and sleep? Birds need to be resilient, as they never know what will happen to their habitat.

A study in *The Auk* showed that wild birds are capable of recovering from stresses experienced early in life, and of going on to reproductive success as adults. [Ref 16-1] Wild baby birds can experience many stresses in their early lives, including sibling competition, extreme weather, and lack of food. Some experiments with birds in captivity had found that increasing early-life stress through food deprivation, elevated stress hormones, and other means had negative effects on birds when they reached adulthood, causing them to have shorter lives and produce fewer offspring.

However, Hugh Drummond and Sergio Ancona—authors of the article in *The Auk*—contended that the artificial stresses created in these experiments were far greater than would ever be experienced by wild birds, and therefore did not reflect what happens in nature. Hugh Drummond conducted long-term observations of Blue-footed Boobies, and found they were resilient to severe stresses in infancy. Boobies that grew up suffering daily oppression by their elder siblings performed as well as those siblings on measures taken during adulthood, including annual survival at all ages, age at first breeding, aggressive defense of offspring, and reproductive success at all ages.

The ornithologist Ludlow Griscom commented on the resilience of birds: (Ref 16-2) "When it comes to death, extraordinary danger, and what human beings would call tragedy, it is astonishing how it all passes in a few minutes, all recollection seems to fade, and apparently no scar of any kind is left."

Griscom described his experience with a robin during World War Two: (Ref 16-3) "In spite of the vivid emotional life of birds, and in spite of their extreme acuity of hearing compared to that of human beings, the degree of their indifference in certain circumstances is positively incredible. In the last world war, there were many observations all going to prove conclusively that the nesting birds in the battle-fronts were much less affected and upset by the shellfire than were the human beings. At one time I was stationed in a small village back of the Second Army Front, and my dugout happened to be facing a little country churchyard with quite a variety of shrubbery. Under the somewhat dreary surroundings I got a certain amount of enjoyment out of a robin redbreast which sang nearly all day long in the shrubbery in this churchyard. On a certain morning the Germans shelled us with 13-inch T.N.T. shells; there was a shell every five minutes for about two and a half hours; the base hospital was struck, various people were killed and wounded, and the survivors cowered in their dugouts, hoping for the best. One of these shells fell right through the roof of the church, blew it apart, and filled the garden with rubbish. Seven minutes after the last shell had fallen the robin redbreast climbed up to the top of one of the remaining bushes and began to sing, recovering from the occasion very much more rapidly that I was able to do myself."

Sometimes birds are capable of making adjustments and adapting when positive changes are made to habitat conditions. There are examples of birds returning to places where they had previously been completely extirpated, once these places were restored and made hospitable again.

An example is the restoration of Crissy Field and the Crissy Field Marsh on the north shore of the City of San Francisco. Prior to the restoration, Crissy Field had served heterogeneous uses. In the 1860's the area contained sand dunes, a large saltwater marsh, and islands. By 1912, the marsh was filled in, and an automobile racetrack was built in preparation for the 1915 Panama-Pacific International Exposition. A grassy meadow was used as a landing strip for early airplanes. In 1935, the airfield was paved over.

By 1994, when the National Park Service took over Crissy Field from the military, the area consisted of a crumbling-asphalt unused airstrip enclosed by chain-linked fencing. This site was unappealing to both people and wildlife.

The National Park Service undertook the restoration of Crissy Field and the creation of the Crissy Field Marsh when it acquired the Presidio. Today, the area includes a 20-acre tidal marsh, the 1.7-mile Golden Gate Promenade along San Francisco Bay, a 28-acre grass field used for daily recreation and large public events, and 16 acres of dune habitat The planners of the recreated marsh hoped to restore the wetlands' biodiversity, including fish, birds, and other small aquatic organisms which had not been seen there since the original marsh was filled in. In November, 1999, a channel was dug to open the marsh to San Francisco Bay, allowing the tide to flow in and out.

Crissy Field Marsh is a combination freshwater and saltwater marsh, one of the richest environments for the creation of biodiversity. The Tennessee Hollow's spring-fed tributaries provide fresh water, while the twice-daily tide brings in salt water from San Francisco Bay and the Pacific Ocean. This coastal wetland system thrives on natural disturbance. Fresh water and storm runoff drain from the land into the marsh, bringing sediment that either settles or is flushed out to the bay. Tides constantly ebb and flow, importing minerals and organic materials. This constant movement and mixing create an opportune environment for a variety of organisms.

Since its restoration, Crissy Field Marsh has become an attractive place for a variety of shorebirds and waterfowl who spend time there at various times of the year. Many species of birds not seen there since the marshland was filled in have returned to use the area. This is an example of the great resilience of birds. Some of the birds are attracted by prey species such as the bay shrimp and Dungeness crab that have also returned.

The author lived in San Francisco from 1988 to 2019 and often went to Crissy Field Marsh. The birds who were in the Marsh varied with the seasons and times of day.

Crissy Field Marsh

At various times the author saw the following species in the Marsh: Long-billed Curlew, Willet, Least Sandpiper, Killdeer, Ruddy Duck, Bufflehead, Belted Kingfisher, Marbled Godwit, Whimbrel, Elegant Tern, Caspian Tern, Black-crowned Night Heron, Great Blue Heron, Snowy Egret, Great Egret, Greater Yellowlegs, Pied-billed Grebe, Western Grebe, Greater Scaup, Red-breasted Merganser, Brown Pelican, White Pelican.

David Attenborough, in *The Life of Birds*, made the following observations: [Ref 16-4] "So where are birds going? More extinctions are certain, as man drives on to conquer the remotest parts of the globe, and populations grow and climate continues to change....But other species of birds will return to old habitats, often with man's help."

However, in his book *A Life on Our Planet: My Witness Statement and A Vision for the Future,* David Attenborough warns that humans are causing an accelerating rate of species extinction and biodiversity loss which if it continues will lead to a much less hospitable world for all living things.

Attenborough says that humans' perception of the world is suffering from a "shifting baseline syndrome" [Ref 16-5]. The concept of what is "normal" or "natural" tends to change over time due to the experiences of subsequent generations. Humans have a capacity to forget, over the generations, how biodiverse a natural environment on Earth could and should be.

Each generation defines normal by what it experiences. Concerning life in the ocean, Attenborough writes that humans judge what the sea can provide by the fish populations they know today, not knowing what these populations once were. They expect less and less from the ocean because they have never known for themselves the riches it once held and what it could again provide.

Attenborough writes: [Ref 16-6] "Since the 1950s, on average, wild animal populations have more than halved. When I look back at my earlier films now, I realize that, although I felt I was out there in the wild, wandering through a pristine natural world, that was an illusion. Those forests and plains and seas were already emptying. Many of the larger animals were already rare. A shifting baseline has distorted our perception of all life on earth. We have forgotten that once there were temperate forests that would take days to traverse, herds of bison that would take four hours to pass, and flocks of birds so vast and dense that they darkened the skies. Those things were normal only a few lifetimes ago. Not any longer. We have become accustomed to an impoverished planet.

We have replaced the wild with the tame. We regard the Earth as our planet, run by humankind for humankind. There is little left for the rest of the living world. The truly wild world—that non-human world—has gone. We have overrun the Earth."

Attenborough states: "We share Earth with the living world—the most remarkable life-support system imaginable, constructed over billions of years. The planet's stability has wavered just as its biodiversity has declined—the two things are bound together. To restore stability to our planet, therefore, we must restore its biodiversity, the very thing we have removed. It is the only way out of this crisis that we ourselves have created. We must rewild the world." [Ref 16-7]

Recent reports document the decreasing numbers of birds. A recent scientific study [Ref 16-8] confirmed a decline of more than 25 percent in North American bird populations since 1970. This means there are nearly three billion fewer birds in North America today than there were just 50 years ago. The study reveals that the wide-spread population declines of birds over the past half-century have resulted in the cumulative loss of billions of breeding individuals across a wide range of species and habitats.

"This was an astounding result, even to us," says lead author and Cornell Lab of Ornithology conservation scientist Ken Rosenberg. [Ref 16-9]

The research team included people from the American Bird Conservancy, Smithsonian Conservation Biology Institute, U.S. Geological Survey, the Canadian Wildlife Service, and other institutions. They analyzed the breeding populations of 529 species by pooling data from the North American Breeding Bird Survey, Audubon's Christmas Bird Count, U.S. Fish and Wildlife Service waterfowl surveys, and ten other datasets. They also analyzed recent data collected by weather radar technology that can track large groups of migrating birds. The study could not capture every North American species. Sea and shorebird data was especially limited.

Multiple factors are responsible for these pervasive losses—habitat loss; environmental factors such as pesticide use, insect declines, and climate change; direct threats such as outdoor cats and glass skyscrapers; and increasing dangers to birds on migration.

The results point to how human influence over the last 50 years has chipped away at bird populations [Ref 16-10], says Nicole Michel, senior quantitative ecologist at the National Audubon Society, who was not an author of the study but provided some underlying data.

The global biodiversity crisis has been concerned with documenting species extinctions. But extinction begins with the loss in abundance of individuals. This decrease in individuals in ecosystems can result in compositional and functional changes of these ecosystems. [Ref 16-11] This loss of bird abundance signals an urgent need to address threats to avert future avifaunal collapse and associated loss of ecosystem integrity, function, and services.

Awareness is the first step in making changes that help birds and ecological systems survive.

Chapter 17 – Be Generous and Tolerant

"Compassion and tolerance are not a sign of weakness, but a sign of strength."

Tenzin Gyatso

"Tolerance is the oil which takes the friction out of life."

Wilbert E. Scheer

"Tolerance always has limits—it cannot tolerate what is itself actively intolerant."

Sidney Hook

"That's what I consider true generosity. You give your all and yet you always feel as if it costs you nothing."

Simone de Beauvoir

"You have not lived today until you have done something for someone who can never repay you."

John Bunyan

"I gave you all my secrets and you lost them all. You lost a lot of things but the treasure of it was in the giving, not the keeping."

Julio Alexi Genao, "When You Were Pixels"

"You cannot do a kindness too soon because you never know how soon it will be too late."

Ralph Waldo Emerson

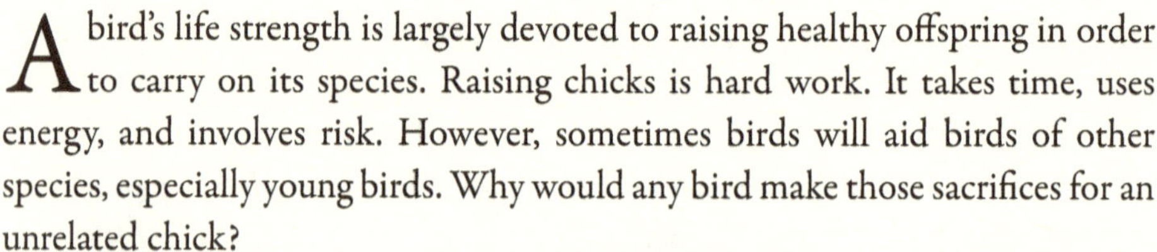

A bird's life strength is largely devoted to raising healthy offspring in order to carry on its species. Raising chicks is hard work. It takes time, uses energy, and involves risk. However, sometimes birds will aid birds of other species, especially young birds. Why would any bird make those sacrifices for an unrelated chick?

There may be a benefit to birds in adopting. Many species of birds that adopt are precocial, meaning that the chicks are mobile and able to feed themselves soon after hatching. Parent ducks, geese, and shorebirds don't feed their chicks, they just lead them to food and protect them. [Ref 17-1] An additional chick doesn't burden the parents much and decreases the chances of a predator's taking one of their own chicks. Many of these species also "creche," or pool several broods of chicks together, caring for them jointly, possibly for exactly these big-brood benefits.

A case where a pooling of offspring seemed to be carried to an extreme was documented by a photographer who saw a female Common Merganser followed by more than 50 ducklings on Lake Bemidji in Minnesota.

FIGURE 17-1 – "MAKE way for dozens and dozens of Common Merganser ducklings. Photo credit: Brent Cizek. (Ref 17-2)

Large brood counts are actually pretty common, said Kenn Kaufman. This is at least partly because ducks often lay their eggs in the nests of other ducks. This behavior doesn't completely explain the photograph, though, because there is a limit to how many eggs one duck can successfully incubate. Female ducks lay about a dozen eggs and can incubate as many as twenty, said Kaufman. More than that, and the birds can't keep all the eggs warm. (Ref 17-3)

The merganser in the picture probably picked up several dozen ducklings that got separated from their mothers. Adult ducks can't tell which birds are theirs, and lost young birds that have already imprinted on their own mothers will instinctively start following another Common Merganser because she looks like their mother.

Birds may adopt for different reasons. In some cases, the parent bird may not realize the additional chick is not its own.

From the perspective of a chick, adoption is usually accidental. Where there are multiple birds breeding close together, it may be hard for the chick and its mother to keep track of each other. For example, Pied Avocet eggs often hatch over two days or more, meaning that some chicks are running around and feeding while others are just hatching. Sometimes the oldest chick will run off to feed with a different group of chicks, and when that group leaves, the chick goes with them. Another possibility is that the parents leave the nest before the youngest chick is ready, and that chick ends up joining another group. [Ref 17-4]

Birds of one species may feed and look after birds of another species. In some cases, one species has brought food to orphaned broods or individuals of another species. This could be triggered by the presumably loud calling of unsatiated youngsters. Examples of such cases include the following: [Ref 17-5]

A brood of Eastern Kingbirds were calling loudly after an electrical storm. The parents were not seen afterward. An Eastern Wood Pewee fed the orphans for ten days, until they fledged. [Ref 17-6]

Black-and-white Warblers fed an Ovenbird fledgling which had become separated from its parents. [Ref 17-7]

A pair of Chipping Sparrows fed a brood of fledgling Purple Finches while continuing to feed their own brood in a nest in a small spruce one tier of branches below the finch nest. [Ref 17-8]

Although a young bird's accepting food no matter who the donor is should be advantageous in most circumstances, being raised by foster parents may lead to later problems. A Mourning Dove remained with its foster family of Ringed Turtle Doves rather than joining its own species. [Ref 17-9] However, the adopted chick had been given a chance to survive.

The noted ornithologist Amelia Laskey (1885 -1973) witnessed birds adopting orphans of different species:

Amelia Laskey (1885 – 1973)

Amelia Laskey published an astonishing 153 papers in ornithological journals. She applied to the United States Fish and Wildlife Service for a banding permit, and from 1931 to 1934 she banded 3,734 birds of 69 species. She began at least three long-range bird life history studies on the Bluebird, the Tufted Titmouse, and the Cardinal, and also conducted a 30-year study of Mockingbirds. [Ref 17-10]

Amelia Laskey's bird banding station became an avian infirmary when local people began bringing her injured and young birds. She was not able to help the sick birds, but the stunned ones recovered quickly after a rest. Those with broken bones she put in a large flying cage with food and water, and they too recovered even though she did not use splints or tapes. "Nature's way of healing is far superior to my inexperienced surgery", she maintained. Amelia raised many nestlings and fledglings herself. Interestingly, she had remarkable success in getting other species of nesting birds to adopt orphaned nestlings. Robins took in a Cardinal. Cardinals looked after Mockingbirds, Bluebirds, and Robins. (Ref 17-11)

Birds' tolerance to other bird species and to the presence of humans varies greatly among individuals of a species and their specific circumstances.

Sometimes, incubating birds will be extremely tolerant of the presence of a human around their nest. A. C. Bent describes the nesting habitats of the Marbled Godwit as follows: (Ref 17-12) "In southwestern Saskatchewan, in 1905 and 1906, I became better acquainted with the Marbled Godwit on its breeding grounds. Along the lower courses of the streams, near the lakes, but sometimes extending for a mile or more back from the lake, are usually found broad, flat, alluvial plains, low enough to be flooded during periods of high water. These plains are more or less moist at all times, are exceedingly level, and are covered with short, thick grass only a few inches high. Such spots are the chosen breeding grounds of the Marbled Godwit, and so far as our experience goes, the nests of this species are invariably placed on these grassy plains or meadows. The Godwit makes no attempt at concealment, the eggs being deposited in plain sight in a slight hollow in the short grass.

On June 9, 1906, I enjoyed a most interesting experience with an unusually tame individual of this normally shy species. While walking across the flat meadow near the creek, I happened to see a Marbled Godwit crouching on her nest beside a pile of horse droppings. She was conspicuous enough in spite of her protective coloration, for the nest was entirely devoid of concealment in the short grass. Though we stood within ten feet of her, she showed no signs of flying away, which suggested the possibility of photographing her. My camera was half a mile away in our wagon, but I soon returned with it and began operations at a distance of fifteen feet, setting up the camera on a tripod and focusing carefully. I moved up cautiously to within ten feet and took another picture, repeating the performance again within five feet. She still sat like a rock, and I made bold to move even closer, spreading the legs of the tripod on either side of her and placing the camera within three feet of her. I hardly dared to breathe, moving very slowly as I used the focusing cloth, and changed my plate holders most cautiously, but she never offered to move and showed not the slightest signs of fear, while I exposed all the plates I had with me, photographing her from both sides and placing the lens within two feet of her. She sat there patiently, panting in the hot sun, apparently distressed by the heat, perhaps partially dazed by it, and much annoyed by the ants which were constantly crawling into her eyes and half open bill, causing her to wink or shake her head occasionally. I reached down carefully and stroked her on the back, but still she did not stir, and I was finally obliged to lift her off the nest in order to photograph the eggs."

The author was impressed by the tolerance of a Long-billed Curlew to other birds and to people at Crissy Field Marsh:

On the way back from my jog, I noticed five crows on the mud bar. They tried to intimidate and distract the Long-billed Curlew so that she would drop her food. They flew directly above her, so that she had to duck her head. One time she went after one of them with her long bill. This was the only time I saw her do anything that approached being aggressive. She was always aware of the other birds in the marsh, but she did not act aggressively towards them nor did she use her long bill to shoo them away. I never saw her use her long sharp bill to dig at other birds (except to point it at a gull if it harassed her). She would walk very close to other birds in her search for food, but she did not try to get them out of her way; rather she would walk around them. I considered her the 'Queen of Crissy Field Marsh' but she did not lord it over other birds or try to intimidate them. I saw her walk near American Coots. Least Sandpipers, and other birds, large and small, but she did not bother them, providing that they did not attack her.

January 6, 2019 was a rainy, windy day. I saw the outline of the male Curlew on the western sandbar and the female Curlew was feeding on the eastern sandbar quite close to me. I watched her dig down and come up with a pinkish item. Then a Ring-billed Gull flew at her from above, and she crouched down. He came after her again before she had a chance to get the food down her long bill. She took off in flight and flew high up with the gull in pursuit right behind her. She flew in a half circle and then suddenly made a sharp turn to try to evade the gull. She flew over me and out towards the bay. Finally, the gull turned back. The Curlew flew around the marsh, coming down lower and landing on the sandbar again. There was nothing in her bill, so I hoped she had been able to swallow the food in flight. Then she resumed feeding.

On December 9, 2018 hundreds of people, dressed in bright red Santa Claus suits, were participating in a race along the Golden Gate Promenade beside the marsh. The male Long-billed Curlew stood at the edge of the marsh and watched this commotion with some interest. But when I went by the female Curlew, I saw that she was completely ignoring all this color and movement of people, and going about her business of foraging for food. I believe she knew the difference between me and the people who were oblivious to her presence in the marsh. I didn't care about what other people thought of me when I stopped to watch her, but I did care about her and what she thought of me.

FIGURE 17-2 – THE FEMALE Long-billed Curlew and her mate (1). Photo by the author.

FIGURE 17-3 – THE FEMALE Long-billed Curlew and her mate (2). Photo by the author.

In conclusion, studying how birds conduct themselves is a worthwhile endeavor. The more one learns about the way birds live, the more one admires them and wants to ensure their long-term survival so they can continue to inspire us with their courage, optimism, beauty, and determination to do their best.

REFERENCES

Ref 1-1 – "How Simple" by P.P. Ramachandran (translated into English by Manu Mangattu, September 2017.

Ref 1-2 – Academy of American Poets, "Hope is the thing with feathers" by Emily Dickinson (1830-1886). https://poets.org/poem/hope-thing-feathers-254.

Ref 2-1 - Vedder, O., Bouwhuis, S., Sheldon, BC (2013). "Quantitative Assessment of the Importance of Phenotypic Plasticity in Adaptation to Climate Change in Wild Bird Populations." PLOS Biol 11(7): e1001603. https://journals.plos.org/plosbiology/article?id=10.1371/journal.pbio.1001605https://doi.org/10.1371/journal pbio.1001605

Ref 2.2 – Walsh, Jennifer et al, "Genomics of rapid ecological divergence and parallel adaptation in four tidal marsh sparrows". Evolution Letters, 2019; DOI: 10.1002/evl3.126.

Ref 2-3 – Cornell University. "Salt regulation among saltmarsh sparrows evolved in four unique ways: Study defines four of nature's solutions to the same problem.". ScienceDaily, 16 July 2019.

Ref 2-4 – Ibid.

Ref 2-5 – Ibid.

Ref 2-6 - United States Fish and Wildlife Service, Shorebird Sister Schools Program, "A Whimbrel Called Hope", https://www.fws.gov/sssp/whimbrels.html. Last updated 24 January 2017.

Ref 2-7 – Ibid.

Ref 2-8 - Watts, Bryan, "Farewell to Hope". The Center for Conservation Biology at the College of William and Mary, 3 April 2019, https://ccbbirds.org/2019/04/03/farewell-to-hope/

Ref 2-9 – Ibid.

Ref 2-10 - Kessler, Cristina and Marcos Castillo, Hope Is Here! New York and the U.S. Virgin Islands: Little Bell Caribbean, 1st edition, 30 November 2013.

Ref 2-11 - The Cornell Lab of Ornithology, Cornell University, "All About Birds: Whimbrel", https://www.allaboutbirds.org/guide/Whimbrel/overview

Ref 2-12 - Lockhart, Jhaneel, "9 Awesome Facts About Bird Migration". Audubon, October 11, 2012. https://www.audubon.org/news/9-awesome-facts-about-bird-migration.

Ref 2-13 - Egevang, Carsten et al, "Tracking of Arctic Terns (Serna paradisaea) reveals longest animal migration". Proceedings of the National Academy of Sciences of the United States of America, February 2, 2010 107 (5) 2078-2081. https://www.pnas.org/content/107/5/2078

Ref 2-14 - Griscom, Ludlow, Modern Bird Study. Cambridge, Massachusetts: Harvard University Press, 1945, page 81-82.

Ref 2-15 – Ibid, page 94.

Ref 2-16 - Ibid, page 87.

Ref 2-17 – Ibid, page 85.

Ref 2-18 - Williams, Dr. Henry Smith, The Private Lives of Birds. New York: National Travel Club, 1939.

Ref 2-19 – Ibid.

Ref 2-20 – Ibid.

Ref 2-21 - Hochbaum, H. Albert, Travels and Traditions of Waterfowl. (Minneapolis: The University of Minnesota Press, 1955), 246.

Ref 2-22 - Hochbaum, H. Albert, To Ride the Wind. Toronto: Richard Bonnycastle, 1973.

Ref 2-23 - "On the Move". Project BEAK (Bird Education and Awareness for Kids) – Adaptations. http://projectbeak.org/adaptations/migration_how2.htm

Ref 2-24 – Ibid.

Ref 2-25 - Deppe, Jill L. et al, "Fat, weather and data affect migratory songbirds' departure decisions, routes, and time it takes to cross the Gulf of Mexico". Proceedings of the National Academy of Sciences of the United States of America, November 17, 2015. 112 (46) E6331-E6338, first published November 2, 2015. https://doi.org/10.1073/pnas.1503381112

Ref 2-26 – Ibid.

Ref 2-27 – Ibid.

Ref 2-28 - Ward, Michael P., et al, "Estimating apparent survival of songbirds crossing the Gulf of Mexico during autumn migration". Proceedings of the Royal Society B Biological Sciences, 24 October, 2018. https://royalsocietypublishing.org/doi/full/10.1098/rspb.2018.1747

Ref 2-29 - Quinn, Lauren, "Plump songbirds more likely to survive migration over Gulf of Mexico". ACES News, College of Agricultural, Consumer & Environmental Sciences, University of Illinois, Urbana Champaign, October 24, 2018. https://aces.illinois.edu/news/plump-songbirds-more-likely-survive-migration-over-gulf-mexico.

Ref 2-30 – Ibid.

Ref 2-31 - "Trans-Gulf Migrants". Texas Parks & Wildlife. https://tpwd.texas.gov/huntwild/wild/birding/migration/transgulf_migrants/

Ref 2-32 -Williams, Dr. Henry Smith, The Private Lives of Birds. New York: National Travel Club, 1939. Page 129.

Ref 2-33 – Ibid, page 17.

Ref 2-34 - Mazarolle, D.F., S.G. Sealy, and K.A. Hobson. 2011. "Inter-annual flexibility in breeding phenology of a neotropical migrant songbird in response to weather conditions at breeding and wintering areas". Écoscience 18:18-25.

Ref 2-35 – Ibid.

Ref 2-36 - Mettke-Hofmann, Claudia, "Curiosity and flexibility help birds to master rapid environmental change". Atlas of Science – another view on science, January 14, 2017. https://atlasofscience.org/curiosity-and-flexibility-help-birds-to-master-rapid-environmental-change/

Ref 2-37 - Inkley, Doug, et al, "Shifting Skies: Migratory Birds in a Warming World". National Wildlife Federation, 2013.

Ref 2-38 - Griscom, Ludlow, Modern Bird Study. Cambridge, Massachusetts: Harvard University Press, 1945, page 159.

Ref 2-39 - Inkley, Doug, et al, "Shifting Skies: Migratory Birds in a Warming World". National Wildlife Federation, 2013.

Ref 2-40 - Griscom, Ludlow, Modern Bird Study. Cambridge, Massachusetts: Harvard University Press, 1945, page 160.

Ref 2-41 - Shankman, Sabrina, "Dead Birds Washing Up by the Thousands Send a Warning About Climate Change." Inside Climate News, 15 January 2020. A new study unravels the mystery of what caused so many of these normally resilient seabirds to starve amid an ocean heat wave fueled in part by global warming. https://insideclimatenews.org/news/15012020/seabird-death-ocean-heat-wave-blob-pacific-alaska-common-murre

Ref 2-42 - Ibid.

Ref 2-43 - Ibid.

Ref 2-44 – Ibid.

Ref 2-45 - Davies, Gareth Huw, "Evolution". In Public Broadcasting System's The Life of Birds by David Attenborough. https://www.pbs.org/lifeofbirds/evolution/index.html

Ref 2-47 - Williams, Dr. Henry Smith, The Private Lives of Birds. New York: National Travel Club, 1939. Page 43.

Ref 3-1 - Compton, Gail, "Compton: Birds on a beach, ready for flight". The St. Augustine Record, March 27, 2010.

Ref 3-2 - Rattenborg, Niels C., Lima, Steven L., and Amlaner, Charles J., "Half-awake to the risk of predation". Nature 397, 397-398 (1999). https://doi.org/10.1038/17037

Ref 3-3 – Ibid.

Ref 4-1 - Greij, Eldon, "Bird basics: Six different feather types explained". Amazing Birds column, January/February 2016. Updated June 28, 2019. https://www.birdwatchingdaily.com/news/science/bird-basics-six-different-feather-types-explained/

Ref 4-2 – Ibid.

Ref 4-3 - Zhao, Jing-Shan et al, "Shaking the wings and preening feathers with the beak help a bird to recover its ruffled feather vane". Materials & Design, February 2020. 187: 108410. doi:10.1016/j.matdes.2019.108410. Located on: https://en.wikipedia.org/wiki/Preening

Ref 4-4 – Ibid.

Ref 4-5 - International Bird Rescue, "How Oil Affects Birds". https://www.birdrescue.org/our-work/research-and-innovation/how-oil-affects-birds/

Ref 4-6 - Williams, Dr. Henry Smith, The Private Lives of Birds. New York: National Travel Club, 1939. Page 218

Ref 4-7 – Ibid, Page 218.

Ref 4-8 – Ibid. Page 243-244

Ref 4-9 - Kaufman, Kenn and Kimberly, "Using Their Senses: Discover the fascinating ways birds survive through sight, sound, taste, touch and smell". Birds and Blooms, October/November, 2018. p 36-41.

Ref 4-10 - "How do Birds See Colour?" BirdSpot – Bird Brains – How do birds see colour? https://www.birdspot.co.uk/bird-brain/how-do-birds-see-colour

Ref 4-11 – Berger, Cynthia, "True Colors: How Birds See the World: Thanks to UV vision, birds see the world very differently than we do." National Wildlife Federation, July 19, 2012. https://www.nwf.org/Magazines/National-Wildlife/2012/AugSept/Animals/Bird-Vision

Ref 4-12 – Ibid.

Ref 4-13 – Ibid.

Ref 4-14 – Barry Jessie, and Marc Devokatis, "Birdwatching Tips: It's Summer…Where Did the Birds Go?" All About Birds, The Cornell Lab, June 1, 2021. https://www.allaboutbirds.org/news/bird-watching-tips-its-summer-where-did-the-birds-go/

Ref 4-15 – "The Basics: Feather Molt". The Cornell Lab, All About Birds, April 20, 2008. https://www.allaboutbirds.org/news/the-basics-feather-molt/

Ref 4-16 – Ibid.

Ref 4-17 – Ibid.

Ref 5-1 - James, Richard, "How Good is the Hearing of the Blue Tit?" Royal Society for the Protection of Birds, Birds and Wildlife, Ask an Expert, April 20, 2011. https://ww2.rspb.org.uk/birds-and-wildlife/bird-and-wildlife-guides/ask-an-expert/previous/bluetit_hearing.aspx

Ref 5-2 - Kaufman, Kenn and Kimberly, "Using Their Senses: Discover the fascinating ways birds survive through sight, sound, taste, touch and smell". Birds and Blooms, October/November, 2018. p 39.

Ref 5-3 - Mayntz, Melissa, "Why Do Birds Sing?" The Spruce, updated January 5, 2020. https://www.thespruce.com/why-birds-sing-386221

Ref 5-4 - Thompson, Mya and Annalyse Moskeland, "How and Why Birds Sing". The Cornell Lab, Bird Academy, August 12, 2014. https://academy.allaboutbirds.org/birdsong/

Ref 5-5 – - Mancini, Mark, "Can Different Bird Species 'Talk' with Each Other?" How Stuff Works, January 12, 2018. http:animals.howstuffworks.com/birds/can-bird-species-talk-with-each-other.htm

Ref 5-6 - "All About Bird Song". The Cornell Lab. https://academy.allaboutbirds.org/features/birdsong/practice-perfect

Ref 5-7 - Naguib, M. and K. Riebel, "Birdsong: A Key Model in Animal Communication—Singing Versatility". Encyclopedia of Language & Linguistics (Second Edition), 2006.

Ref 5-8 – Ibid.

Ref 5-9 – Ibid.

Ref 5-10 – Ibid.

Ref 5-11 - "Birds have regional accents according to scientists." Bill Turnbull and Sian Williams report, BBC News, 13 December 2011. https://www.bbc.com/news/av/science-environment-16154490

Ref 5-12 - Thompson, Mya and Annalyse Moskeland, "How and Why Birds Sing". The Cornell Lab, Bird Academy, August 12, 2014. https://academy.allaboutbirds.org/birdsong/

Ref 5-13 - Eck, Allison, "What Birdsong Can Teach Us About Creativity: The way birds construct their songs could give us insight into the nature of creativity and the learning process". Nova, Public Broadcasting System, Wednesday, April 9, 2014.

Ref 6-1 - Thompson, Joanna, "A Drone Crash Caused Thousands of Elegant Terns to Abandon Their Nests: California wildlife managers are hoping the birds relocated to other nesting sites. Meanwhile, they are working to ensure this doesn't happen again." Audubon Magazine, June 11, 2021. https://www.audubon.org/news/a-drone-crash-caused-thousands-elegant-terns-abandon-their-nests

Ref 6-2 – Ibid.

Ref 6-3 – Ibid.

Ref 6-4 – Curtis, Russ, "Thousands of Seabirds Saved in Long Beach Harbor With Innovation and Hard Work". International Bird Rescue, July 29, 2021.

Ref 6-5 – Curtis, Russ and J.D. Bergeron, "Southern California Seabird Rescue Continues to Evolve, 500 Elegant Tern Chicks Admitted." International Bird Rescue, July 20, 2021.

Ref 6-6 – Curtis, Russ, "Update: Hundreds of Seabirds Released, 105 Elegant Tern Critical Patients Still in Care". International Bird Rescue, August 12, 2021.

Ref 6-7 – Curtis, Russ, "A Story of Hope: 'Little Mike' Tiniest Seabird Survivor Stands Out Among 467 Rescued Elegant Terns." International Bird Rescue, July 16, 2021.

Ref 6-8 - Johnson, Allison E., Christina Masco, and Stephen Pruett-Jones, "Song Recognition and Heterospecific Associations Between Two Fairy Wren Species (Maluridae)". Behavioral Ecology, 2018; DOI: 10.1093/beheco/ary071

Ref 6-9 - "Birds from different species recognize each other and cooperate". Science Daily, May 21, 2018. Source: University of Chicago Medical Center. https://www.sciencedaily.com/releases/2018/05/180521143827.htm

Ref 6-10 - Dugger, B.D., and K.M. Duffer, 2002. "Long-billed curlew (Numenius americanus). Species Account Number 628. The Birds of North America Online (A. Poole, Ed.) Ithaca: Cornell Lab of Ornithology.

Ref 6-11 - Bent, A. C., Life Histories of North American Shore Birds – Part II. United States Government Printing Office. Smithsonian Institution United States National Museum Bulletin 146.

Ref 6-12 - Smithsonian Institution Archives, Record Unit 7120, Bent, Arthur Cleveland, 1866-1954, Arthur Cleveland Bent Papers, circa 1910-1954 Collection Overview. https://siarchives.si.edu/collections/siris_arc_217278

Ref 6-13 – Ibid.

Ref 6-14 - Bent, A. C., Life Histories of North American Shore Birds, Part II, originally published in 1929 as Smithsonian Institution United States National Museum Bulletin 146. New York: Dover Publications, Inc. page 9.

Ref 6-15 – Silling, Celest, "Why Birds Flock". Gulf Coast Bird Observatory. https://www.gcbo.org/wp-content/uploads/2020/01/Flock-Nature-Notes.pdf

Ref 6-16 – Ibid.

Ref 6-17 – Ibid.

Ref 6-18 - Beauchamp, Guy, "Diving Behavior in Surf Scoters and Barrow's Goldeneyes". The Auk, 109(4):819-827, 1992.

Ref 7-1 - Williams, Dr. Henry Smith, The Private Lives of Birds. New York: National Travel Club, 1939.

Ref 7-2 - "Survival by the numbers". Bird Academy, The Cornell Lab. https://academy.allaboutbirds.org

Ref 7-3 - The Cornell Lab, All About Birds, "What's Going On When I See Little Birds Going After A Big Bird?". April 1, 2009. https://www.allaboutbirds.org/news/sometimes-i-see-little-birds-going-after-a-big-bird-why-do-they-do-this/

Ref 7-4 - Bent, Arthur Cleveland, Life Histories of North American Shore Birds, Part II. Originally published in 1929 as Smithsonian Institution United States National Museum Bulletin 146. New York: Dover Publications, Inc., 1962. Page 92

Ref 7-5 – Ibid, page 101-102.

Ref 7-6 - Ellison, Kevin and Ribic, Christine, "Nest Defense – Grassland Bird Responses to Snakes" (2012). USGS Northern Prairie Wildlife Research Center. 252. https://digitalcommons.unl.edu/usgsnpwrc/252

Ref 8-1 - McClain, Joe. "Winnie the Whimbrel: RIP". William and Mary News & Media, September 9, 2008, https://www.wm.edu/news/stories/2008/winnie-is-down-3006.php (accessed July 23, 2020).

Ref 8-2 - Watts, Bryan. "Mackenzie Whimbrels Complete Loop Migration". The Center for Conservation Biology, William & Mary and Virginia Commonweath University, July 15, 2013, https://ccbbirds.org/2013/07/15/mackenzie-whimbrels-complete-loop-migration/ (accessed July 23, 2020).

Ref 9-1 - Kaye, Steve, "The First Choice You Make". November 2018. Steve Kaye blog. https://www.stevekaye.com/choice/

Ref 9-2 - Beeley, Fergus and Matt Hamilton (Directors) & Kaufman, Fred (Producer) & Male, Michael and Neil Rettig (Photography) (2012). "Magic of the Snowy Owl" [DVD]. Public Broadcasting System, Nature.

Ref 10-1 - Kaufman, Kenn, Lives of North American Birds. New York: Houghton Mifflin Company, 1996. Page 52.

Ref 10-2 - Januszkiewicz, Eric, "Patience is a Virtue Among Herons". Wild View, An Eye on Wildlife, August 24, 2018. https://blog.wcs.org/photo/2018/08/24/patience-is-a-virtue-among-herons-bird-florida/

Ref 10-3 - Bent, A.C., Life Histories of North American Marsh Birds. Smithsonian Institution, United States National Museum Bulletin 135. (Washington, D.C.: United States Government Printing Office, March 11, 1927), 101-114.

Ref 10-4 – Ibid.

Ref 10-5 - Merriam, Florence A., A-Birding on a Bronco. Boston: Houghton, Mifflin and Company, The Riverside Press, Cambridge, 1896.

Ref 10-6 - Liao, Kristine, "How Orioles Build Those Incredible Hanging Nests: The delicate-looking structures are stronger than they seem, and come in a variety of shapes and materials". Audubon News, August 6, 2019. https://www.audubon.org/news/how-orioles-build-those-incredible-hanging-nests

Ref 10-7 – Ibid.

Ref 10-8 - Gliozzo, Joe, "Arctic Angels on the Dunes: How to Photograph Snowy Owls". Destination Wildlife, February 6, 2018.

Ref 10-9 - Baldwin, Emma. "Patience Taught By Nature by Elizabeth Barrett Browning". Poem Analysis. https://poemanalysis.com/elizabeth-barrett-browning/patience-taught-by-nature/. Accessed 5 June 2021.

Ref 11-1 - "Loon, Loons and More Loons". Views From the Top – forum – General Backcountry, post by stopher. https://www.vftt.org/forums/showthread.php?37462-Loon-Loons-and-more-Loons

Ref 11-2 – Ibid.

Ref 11-3 - Bent, Arthur Cleveland. Life Histories of North American Diving Birds: Order Pygopodes. Smithsonian Institution, United States National Museum Bulletin 107. (Washington, D.C.: United States Government Printing Office, 1919), 47-60.

Ref 11-4 – Ibid, page 56.

Ref 11-5 – Ibid, page 58.

Ref 11-6 - Tukua, Deborah, "5 Fascinating Facts About Ravens". Farmer's Almanac, updated December 5, 2020. https://www.farmersalmanac.com/fascinating-facts-about-ravens-22850

Ref 11-7 - Mayntz, Melissa, "Birds at Play". The Spruce, May 28, 2019. https://www.thespruce.com/birds-at-play-386461

Ref 11-8 - Emery, Nathan J., and Clayton, Nicola S., "Do birds have the capacity for fun?" Current Biology, Volume 25, Issue 1, 5 January 2015, pages R15-R20. https://doi.org/10.1016/j.cub.2014.09.020

Ref 12-1 - Peterson, Christine, "Birds that Carry Lit Candles & The Importance of Avian Innovation." Cool Green Science, April 15, 2020. https://blog.nature.org/science/2020/04/15/birds-that-carry-lit-candles-the-importance-of-avian-innovation/

Ref 12-2 - Eck, Allison, "What Birdsong Can Teach Us About Creativity: The way birds construct their songs could give us insight into the nature of creativity and the learning process". Nova, Public Broadcasting System, Wednesday, April 9, 2014.

Ref 12-3 – Ibid.

Ref 12-4 – Ibid.

Ref 12-5 - Farnsworth, G., G.A. Londono, J.V. Martin, K.C. Derrickson, and R. Breitwisch (2020). Northern Mockingbird (Mimus polyglottos), version 1.0. In Birds of the World (A.F. Poole, Editor). Cornell Lab of Ornithology, Ithaca, NY, USA. https://doi.org/10.2173/bow.normoc.01 https://birdsoftheworld.org/bow/species/normoc/1.0/introduction

Ref 12-6 - Williams, Dr. Henry Smith, The Private Lives of Birds. New York: National Travel Club, 1939. Page 118-119.

Ref 12-7 – Ibid, Page 122.

Ref 12-8 – Ibid, Page 128.

Ref 13-1 - Griscom, Ludlow, Modern Bird Study. Cambridge, Massachusetts: Harvard University Press, 1945, page 34.

Ref 13-2 - Watanabe, S., Sakamoto, J., Wakita, M., "Pigeons' discrimination of paintings by Monet and Picasso". Journal of the Experimental Analysis of Behavior, 1995 March 63(2): 165-174. DOI: 10,1901/jeab.1995.63-165.

Ref 13-3 - Clayton, Nicola; Emery, Nathan & Dickinson, Anthony (2006). "The rationality of animal memory: Complex caching strategies of western scrub jays". In Hurley, Susan & Nudds, Matthew (eds.). Rational Animals? Oxford University Press. pp.197–216.

Ref 13-4 - Clayton, N. S.; Dally, J. M. & Emery, N. J. (2007)."Social cognition by food-caching corvids. The western scrub-jay as a natural psychologist". Philosophical Transactions of the Royal Society of London. Series B, Biological Sciences.362(1480): 507–22

Ref 13-5 - Bent, Arthur Cleveland, Life Histories of North American Shore Birds, Part II. Originally published in 1929 as Smithsonian Institution United States National Museum Bulletin 146. New York: Dover Publications, Inc., 1962. Page 166.

Ref 13-6 - Thorpe, William Homan, Learning and Instinct in Animals. London: Methuen, 1963, 2nd edition.

Ref 13-7 - Jarvis, E., Güntürkün, O., Bruce, L. et al. Avian brains and a new understanding of vertebrate brain evolution. Nature Reviews Neuroscience 6, 151–159 (2005). https://doi.org/10.1038/nrn1606

Ref 13-8 - Stretka, Bret, "Bird Brains Are Far More Humanlike Than Once Thought". Scientific American, September 24, 2020.

Ref 13-9 - Stacho M, Herold C, Rook N, Wagner H, Axer M, Amunts K, Güntürkün O. "A cortex-like canonical circuit in the avian forebrain". Science. 2020 Sep 25;369(6511):eabc5534. DOI:10.1126/science.abc5534

Ref 13-10 - Olkowicz, S., et al. (2016). "Birds have primate-like numbers of neurons in the forebrain". Proceedings of the National Academy of Sciences of the United States, June 13, 2016. DOI: 10.1073/pnas.1517131113

Ref 13-11 - National Science Foundation News Release 05-010, "Scientists Propose Sweeping Changes to Naming of Bird Neurosystems to Acknowledge Their True Brainpower: Researchers now see birds' cognitive ability as more comparable to mammals". https://www.nsf.gov/news/news_images.jsp?cntn_id=100744&org=NSF

Ref 14-1 - Mayntz, Melissa, "Do Birds Mate for Life?" The Spruce, October 12, 2019. https://www.thespruce.com/do-birds-mate-for-life-386725

Ref 14-2 - Berger, Michele, "Till Death Do Them Part: 8 Birds that Mate for Life". Audubon News, February 10, 2012. https://www.audubon.org/news/till-death-do-them-part-8-birds-mate-life

Ref 14-3 – Ibid.

Ref 14-4 – Ibid.

Ref 14-5 – Ibid.

Ref 14-6 – Ibid.

Ref 14-7 - Hoskins, Rachel, "Which birds mate for life? And birds' mating rituals", Woodland Trust Org., 14 Feb 2020. https://www.woodlandtrust.org.uk/blog/2020/02/which-birds-mate-for-life/

Ref 14-8 - Harrison, George, "Do Birds Mate for Life?". Birds & Blooms, originally published 15 September 2013; updated 24 April 2020.

Ref 14-9 - "Ten fascinating facts about WWT founder Sir Peter Scott". Posted on 09 December 2019. Wildfowl & Wetlands Trust. https://www.wwt.org.uk/news-and-stories/news/ten-fascinating-facts-about-sir-peter-scott/

Ref 14-10 - "Slimbridge News - Bewick's swans update". Posted on 11 January 2021. Wildfowl & Wetlands Trust. https://www.wwt.org.uk/wetland-centres/slimbridge/news/swan-news

Ref 15-1 – "Snowy Owl (Bubo scandiacus) – Facts and Adaptations". Cool Antarctica.

Ref 15-2 - Watson, Adam, "The Behaviour, Breeding, and Food Ecology of the Snowy Owl Nyctea Scandiaca." Ibis, International Journal of Avian Science, Volume 99, Issue 3, July 1957, pages 419-462.

Ref 15-3 - Beeley, Fergus and Matt Hamilton (Directors) & Kaufman, Fred (Producer) & Male, Michael and Neil Rettig (Photography) (2012). "Magic of the Snowy Owl" [DVD]. Public Broadcasting System, Nature.

Ref 15-4 - "Acceptance, by Robert Frost". https://www.robertfrost.org/acceptance.jsp

Ref 16-1 - Drummond, Hugh & Ancona, Sergio (2015). "Observational field studies reveal wild birds responding to early-life stresses with resilience, plasticity, and intergenerational effects". The Auk.132.563-576. 10.1642/AUK-14-244.1.

Ref 16-2 - Griscom, Ludlow, Modern Bird Study. Cambridge, Massachusetts: Harvard University Press, 1945, page 27-28

Ref 16-3 – Ibid.

Ref 16-4 - Davies, Gareth Huw, "Evolution". Public Broadcasting Service: The Life of Birds by David Attenborough. http://www.pbs.org/lifeofbirds/evolution/index.html

Ref 16-5 – Attenborough, David, A Life on Our Planet: My Witness Statement and A Vision for the Future. New York: Grand Central Publishing, Hachette Book Group, 2020, Page 237.

Ref 16-6 – Ibid, Page 100.

Ref 16-7 – Ibid.

Ref 16-8 – Rosenberg, Kenneth V. et al, "Decline of the North American avifauna." Science, 04 October 2019. Vol. 366, Issue 6461. DOI:10.1126/science.aaw/1313. Page 120-124.

Ref 16-9 – Mock. Jillian, "North America Has Lost More Than 1 in 4 Birds in Last 50 Years, New Study Says." Audubon News, September 19, 2019. https://www.audubon.org/news/north-america-has-lost-more-1-4-birds-last-50-years-new-study-says

Ref 16-10 – Ibid.

Ref 16-11 – Rosenberg, Kenneth V. et al, "Decline of the North American avifauna." Science, 04 October 2019. Vol. 366, Issue 6461. DOI:10.1126/science.aaw/1313. Page 120-124.

Ref 17-1 - "Adoption in birds (really!)". Tough Little Birds. Posted on January 23, 2014. https://toughlittlebirds.com/2014/01/23/adoption-in-birds-really/

Ref 17-2 - Mock, Julian, "Here's Why This Mama Merganser Has More Than 50 Ducklings: A photographer in Minnesota recently captured an adorable shot of a Common Merganser followed by dozens of fuzzy babies". Audubon News, July 13, 2018. https://www.audubon.org/news/heres-why-mama-merganser-has-more-50-ducklings

Ref 17-3 – Ibid.

Ref 17-4 - "Adoption in birds (really!)". Tough Little Birds. Posted on January 23, 2014. https://toughlittlebirds.com/2014/01/23/adoption-in-birds-really/

Ref 17-5 - Shy, Marilyn Muszalski, "Interspecific Feeding Among Birds: A Review". Journal of Field Ornithology, Autumn 1982. 53(4):370-393.

Ref 17-6 - Snyder, W. E. 1913. "The wood pewee as a foster parent". Auk 30:273.

Ref 17-7 - Kendeigh, S.C. 1945. "Nesting behavior of wood warblers". Wilson Bulletin. 57:145-164.

Ref 17-8 - Jackson, R.E. 1941. "Song Sparrows assume role of foster parents". Bulletin of the. Massachusetts Audubon Society 25:134-135.

Ref 17-9 - Grewe, A. 1959. "Ring Doves rear Mourning Doves". Flicker 31:24

Ref 17-10 - Bonta, Marcia Myers. Women in the Field – America's Pioneering Women Naturalists. College Station, Texas: Texas A & M University Press, 1991, 232-233.

Ref 17-11 – Ibid, 234.

Ref 17-12 - Bent, A. C., Life History of North American Shore Birds, Order Limicolae (Part I). Smithsonian Institution, United States National Museum Bulletin No. 142 (Washington, D.C.: United States Government Printing Office, 1927), 280.

ABOUT THE AUTHOR

VAL SHUSHKEWICH (NÉE Cuffe) has a life-long fascination with the lives of birds. Research and writing are her personal interests, especially in the world of nature and birds.

She has a Master of Business Administration from the University of Toronto, is a Chartered Financial Analyst (CFA), and works as a financial analyst.

PUBLISHED BOOKS

THE REAL WINNIE: A ONE-OF-A-KIND BEAR. Toronto: Natural Heritage Books, 2003; second printing 2005. There are Japanese and Czechoslovakian editions of this book.

This is the true story of the real black bear who was the inspiration for the Winnie the Pooh stories. While visiting Assiniboine Park Zoo with her parents in Winnipeg, Manitoba, Val was captivated by the statue of a soldier and a small bear cub. The soldier was Harry Colebourn, a veterinarian with the Fort Garry Horse cavalry regiment and part of the Canadian Expeditionary Force of World War One. He had rescued the orphaned black bear cub and named her Winnipeg, or Winnie for short. Winnie accompanied the regiment to training grounds in England and then was taken to the London Zoo when Harry was ordered to the front lines in France. Winnie was an extraordinary bear who became a star attraction at the London Zoo. A. A. Milne's son, Christopher, loved to visit her, and Winnie became immortalized in the Winnie the Pooh stories.

MORE THAN BIRDS: ADVENTUROUS LIVES OF NORTH AMERICAN NATURALISTS. Toronto: Dundurn Press, 2012.

This book follows the development of bird natural history studies in North America through the life stories of 22 naturalists.

A reviewer in GoodReads said this about *More Than Birds – Adventurous Lives of North American Naturalists*: "I picked up this book because I was interested in only a couple of the mini biographies of well-known naturalists, but I ended up reading almost the entire book. Shushkewich has a writing style that is clear, easy to read, and she manages to delve into details of lives and research while managing to stay succinct. As a result, the biographies kept my interest, and I was thoroughly engaged."

The 1800s saw early North American naturalists describing and illustrating the spectacular flora and fauna they found in the New World. Then collectors and scientists of the Smithsonian Institution and the Canadian Museum of Nature worked feverishly to describe and catalogue the species that exist on the continent. After that came the naturalists who were interested in describing the lives of the birds.

Early conservationists were instrumental in the creation of great bird sanctuaries. The emphasis of today's naturalists, including Robert Nero, Robert Bateman, Kenn Kaufman, and David Allen Sibley, is to do everything then can to encourage people to experience nature and wildlife directly in their lives. The hope is that once people encounter the natural world more and become aware of its beauty, intricacy, and fragility, they will want to protect and preserve it.

ARCTIC CHANGES: PAST TO PRESENT IN THE FAR NORTH. Draft2Digital, 2021.

This is an educational and entertaining book that persuades readers to think about and take seriously the changes that are occurring in the Arctic. It combines descriptions of what the Arctic was like in the past and its historical explorations, with the enormous changes that have happened and that are continuing to unfold. Major developments that scientists and indigenous peoples are currently trying to understand and deal with are described. The focus is on the changes – old to new conditions – in the far north.

The book entertains with stories about Arctic heroes and animal rescues. Readers of this book will gain an understanding of how warming is changing the lives of people, animals, and birds living in the Arctic.

CLOSE ENCOUNTERS OF THE BIRD KIND: WILD BIRDS IN SAN FRANCISCO AND OTHER PLACES. Draft2Digital, 2021.

This book describes adventures with birds in San Francisco and other places, involving photography, habitat restoration, and rescue attempts. It follows the experiences of a bird lover and naturalist in places that are very wild, and yet are within walking distance of highly urban centers. The life habits of the birds are described, as well as the effect the birds have on the author.

The author's study and love of birds led her to volunteer in the baby bird room at WildCare, a rescue and rehabilitation center in San Rafael, California. She also received training from the Oiled Wildlife Care Network. In the devastating 2007 Cosco Busan oil spill in San Francisco Bay, which affected thousands of migrating and overwintering birds, she was able to help in efforts to save oiled birds at the worldwide-known International Bird Rescue center in Cordelia, California.

<u>PIONEERING ORNITHOLOGISTS</u>. Draft2Digital, 2023.

Discover how the science of ornithology developed by looking at the lives of 20 famous ornithologists. Entire books have been written about many of these intriguing people. The book is approximately 390 pages.

The book has four parts:

- Early Explorers (Georg Wilhelm Steller, William Bartram, Meriwether Lewis, Sir John Richardson);

- Early Ornithology (James Graham Cooper, Joel Asaph Allen, Elliott Ladd Coues, William Dutcher, William Brewster);

- Transition to Modern Ornithology (Frank Michler Chapman, Witmer Stone, Arthur Cleveland Bent, William Leon Dawson, Louis Agassiz Fuertes);

- Modern Ornithology (Rudolph Martin Anderson, Arthur Augustus Allen, Alexander Wetmore, Ludlow Griscom, Terence Michael Shortt, Ernst Walter Mayr).